THE
BLACK KNIGHT'S
Tune

❧ NOVELLA ONE ❧

NAOMI FINLEY

ISBN: 978-1-989165-08-9

Cover designer: Victoria Cooper Art
Website: www.facebook.com/VictoriaCooperArt

Editor: Scripta Word Services
Website: scripta-word-services.com

OTHER BOOKS BY
NAOMI FINLEY

A Slave of the Shadows: Book One

A Guardian of Slaves: Book Two

Novella Series

The Black Knight's Tune: Ruby's Story

The Master of Ships: Charles's Story (coming May 2019)

✑ CHAPTER ✑
One

New York, 1853

I DREAMED OF HIM...THE BLACK KNIGHT AND THE KEEPER OF the tune.

Since Willow Hendricks walked into the restaurant two years ago, the recurring dream had plagued me...

In the darkness of the belly of a ship, a child sits with her knees drawn snuggly to her chest, her face buried in the fabric of her white nightgown. Soft sobs rack her young body.

"Don't weep, little one; I'm here." His voice strums like music notes. The touch of his gentle fingers on her arm—my arm—sends a shudder through me.

I dab my tears with the lace cuff of my nightgown. "I'm scared!" I say, my voice resembling that of a small child.

"Everything be all right." He caresses my cheek with his knuckles and begins to sing the same nostalgic tune.

I sniffle, grasping for the comfort his presence often brings. I rub my eyes with the backs of my hands to part the mist clouding his features.

Then a portal in the floor above opens and I lift an arm to shield my eyes from the blinding light enveloping us. I squint up at the swirling layers of green taffeta in the woman's gown as she floats toward us. Her long chestnut tresses whip around her like ropes. It's her, the regal woman with the mysterious green eyes. I watch, spellbound.

She reaches out her slender hand and curls her finger, summoning the black knight. Her smile is alluring and pure as she looks at him.

He glances back at me, his face drawn and weary. Does she haunt him as she does me? He stretches out his dark hand and her ivory fingers lace through his. Together they ascend like angels and the heavens scoop them up.

Again, the ship's cargo hold goes dark. Cold. Frightening.

"A handkerchief for the lady?" A wee voice shattered my recollection of the dream.

I looked down into the pleading dark eyes of a little girl, only four or five years of age. They were sunk like two black pebbles in her gaunt face. The sting of the cold January morning reddened the fingers holding out the beige cloth. I smiled and bent to be on eye level with her. Removing my glove, I slid my fingers into the hidden pocket in the folds of my russet calico gown. My fingers touched the chilled blade concealed along with the few coins I brought for the child beggars, who often approached me when I visited the Five Points. One could never be too careful when venturing into a place like the slums in lower Manhattan.

I placed the coin in her dirty upturned palm. "You keep the handkerchief for your next customer."

Instinctively, her fingers curled tightly around the coin, concealing it from prying eyes. "Thank you, miss." She grinned and darted off, as quickly as she'd appeared.

Replacing my glove, I adjusted the basket on the

crook of my arm and continued. I turned down Orange Street toward Mary Kelly's tenement. The Irish lady had come to America after the potato famine in the '40s with her husband. His involvement in the riot at the Aster Place in '49 left her a widow with half a dozen children ranging from five years to eleven.

On the corner of Cross and Orange Streets, the sweet voices of the trios of child musicians filtered through the traffic and murmurs of morning activity. Children of all ages roamed the streets to earn whatever coin they could to help feed their families, a sight all too familiar in the Points.

A hansom cab passed me. Inside the carriage the black curtains were pulled back, and a small girl dressed in the finest fashions pressed her nose against the window. She and her gentrified family were one group of the many tourists who increasingly visited the slums. Instead of aiding the people and helping them to apply change to better themselves, people from far and wide thrived on the corruption and destruction and other unfathomable ordeals that took place. Newspapers glorified the area, and people reveled in the stories. The hardworking Irish, freed slaves, Italians, and other immigrants living in the slums became invisible to onlookers.

Misery, sickness, and disease paved the alleyways and streets, and despite the countless times I'd walked them, I'd never allowed myself to become complacent to the pain and suffering.

I turned into a narrow alley, my boots crunching on the snow-covered ground. My heart sped up with the usual fear I felt when I left the main streets. On several occasions, I'd witnessed what happened in the shadowed alleyways in the Points.

On the back stoop of a bordello, a drunken white man lay facedown in a frozen puddle of his vomit. Beside him, a man of color sat with his back against the brothel wall and his legs sprawled out before him, a jug of whiskey teetering on his lap. He turned his head at the sound of my approach. His eyes looked through me as he raised the jug in greeting. "Morning," he said with an intoxicated grin. The jug appeared too heavy for him as he attempted to toss back another drink; it bypassed his lips altogether and he dropped the jug back into his lap.

Pulling my gray woolen coat snuggly around me, I clutched the basket on my arm and hurried past. The frigid wind rustled my dress and crept beneath the layers of fabric to bite at the flesh through my wool stockings.

The two-story tenement at the end of the alley housed hundreds of tenants, but was suitable for scarcely that amount. I pushed on the heavy planked door dangling from the doorjamb on its one hinge and climbed the dark stairway to the third floor, testing my footing on each step to make sure it wouldn't give way and plunge me to the main level.

"That you, Ruby?" Mary called out when I rapped on her door minutes later.

"Yes."

I heard the troubling cough of her seven-year-old daughter through the thin walls. The girl had come down with a temperature four days ago. I'd been by to check on her and brought broth for the girl and dried provisions for the family.

Mary was a seamstress who sewed shirts for men at a base wage. Due to her daughter's illness she'd fallen behind on her quota, which meant the family would not have the money to make rent. The gnawing pain of hunger was no stranger to them.

My parents and I didn't move in prestigious circles, but to them, life hadn't been about climbing an invisible ladder to be accepted by the aristocracy of New York. They taught me to appreciate and give to the ones in need—with the belief that one never knows when their fortune in life could change. My family had never gone without the necessities of life, but with my parents' dedication to the abolitionist movement we'd never acquired wealth, and I continued to be grateful for the simple life we led.

"Well…are you coming?" Mary stood staring at me from the open doorway. Tiny red ribbons traced across her eyes from lack of sleep and shed tears. Her light brown hair hung in a long braid over her reedy shoulder. She pulled her knitted shawl tighter over her patched and threadbare blue dress as the wind seeped in from the broken window in the dim hallway.

Another fit of coughs came from within.

"She isn't any better than she was yesterday?" I entered the one-room apartment and regarded the small figure lying under a flimsy gray blanket. The room's small window, like the window in the hall, was broken and Mary's oldest child, a son, had boarded it up with wood to keep out the cold.

"Fever won't break." Worry hauled at her voice. She closed the door before coming to stand beside me, scratching mindlessly at the rash that'd recently spread up her arms.

"You mustn't dig, or you will get an infection." I set my basket on the makeshift table made of an old door and two crates that stood against the wall to my left and removed my velvet bonnet. Lifting the cloth covering the basket, I removed the jar of my mother's broth, a recipe I'd sipped on many sick days in my life. At the hearthstone, I removed the iron pot hanging on a hook fixed to the wooden plank wall and filled it with some broth. The fire had died; only a few red coals remained.

"We must get this fire going." I set the pot in the coals, hoping to at least take the chill off the liquid.

"My boy's out scavenging for bits of wood. If the sickness doesn't take her, the cold will." Mary moved to the bottom berth of the three-high bunk beds. "If my fool man hadn't gone and gotten himself killed, I wouldn't be left to be the sole moneymaker, and I'd be able to care for Colleen properly." She lifted the limp hand of the frail girl sunken into the straw-tick mattress. She resembled a child half her age.

Gathering my basket, I joined her and lowered myself down onto the edge of the bed. Removing a jar of water and a clean cloth, I dampened the fabric and glided it over the child's forehead and the hot flesh of her face and throat. "What did the doctor Mr. Reed sent by say?"

"He suggested bloodletting her to drain the pneumonia from her body. And I sent him on his way soon after," she said firmly, pressing her lips together. "I wasn't about to let him practice his barbaric ways on my girl." She pressed her daughter's fingers to her lips, worry creasing her pale face. Her own fingers were marred and pricked from her needlework, and deep cracks riddled her knuckles.

After her son returned with a few pieces of wood he'd conjured up, the chill in the room soon subsided.

I filled a wooden bowl with broth and brought it to Mary, who sat with her daughter's head cradled to her breast. "Bless you." She reached for the bowl.

"I need to get going. Mr. Reed will be expecting me at the office."

"Tell the man I thank him for his generosity."

"I will. Stay strong. The children need you."

Her lips quivered, and she beseeched me with hollow eyes. "Please come back."

"I will." I walked to the makeshift table. "My mother sent some wool socks for you and the children, among other things." From inside the basket I took out the socks, a bottle of preserved peaches, a loaf of bread, some salted pork and apples, and ointment for her rash.

Tears tattered her voice. "I can't thank you enough for what you've done for us."

Replacing my bonnet, I smiled at her. "Thank me by taking care of yourself as well."

Succumbing to a flood of tears, she bobbed her head up and down in agreement.

Outside in the alley, I made my way to the front street. Each time I walked the streets, I recalled the short time I'd lived in the Five Points with the Irish boy, Will. Together as children, we'd hidden among the cargo of the ship on our journey to New York. Time had blurred my memories, but the vividness of his ginger hair and the safety I'd felt when he'd been around remained.

The day the men had tried to apprehend us in our shelter, he'd fought them and told me to run. And run I had. Leaving him to fend for himself and filling me with a lifetime of guilt. For years I searched each red-haired boy for the face of my friend, and every time a little piece of me died.

I had received my one miracle in life, and that was the day I ran into Amy Stewart, my adoptive mother, in the market, days before a cholera outbreak ripped through the Five Points and New York.

CHAPTER
Two

A RIPPLING OF WARMTH GREETED ME WHEN I OPENED THE door to the *Manhattan Observer* office and stepped inside. A gust of wintry air swept across the room, fluttering papers on desks and causing a shiver to surge through the staff. For a brief few seconds, the chatter in the main office paused as workers glanced up from their work at my arrival. I swiftly closed the door, and the buzzing of worker bees occupied the room once more.

"Ahh, Ruby, good morning," Kipling said, handing a young boy and his little sister a bundle of that day's newspaper. The children—news hawkers—belonged to Mrs. Kelly; after my pleading with Kipling, he'd given them the job.

I waved a greeting and hung my coat and bonnet on the peg by the window that ran the length of one wall.

Kipling had gone back to giving the children instructions. From my position at the door, I studied the way he gently gripped the russet-haired boy's puny shoulder as he spoke, and the encouraging smile planted on his mouth. The boy's twig-like, dark-haired sister peered up at Kipling with large innocent eyes.

The *Manhattan Observer* was a penny newspaper with a strong focus on its motto: Freedom for All. The pricing of the paper ensured that Kipling's readers were middle- and working-class. Now employing thirty, in the beginning the staff had consisted of Kipling and me. He'd hired me for a wage equivalent to that of a man. His willingness to consider me a man's equal—in smarts alone—had opened my eyes to the quality of the man I called my boss and eventually my friend.

"How's the girl today?" Kipling asked as I joined him and the children, whom he gave a gentle nudge toward the front door.

They hurried their steps and exited the building. I watched them through the large front window—stamped with the name of the newspaper in bright yellow script— until they disappeared into the crowd of New Yorkers hustling up and down the forever humming streets.

"She's the same. Fever hasn't broken." I strode to my desk and sat down.

Saul, the editor in chief, exited his office with a stack of newsprint in hand. His warm amber eyes brushed over my face as he held out the papers. "Run your sharp eyes over these," he said, his voice deep, rich, and most pleasing to the ear. When he spoke, I often imagined him as a singer in a grand opera house, selling out seats night after night—if such a thing was permitted for a person of color.

He made it no secret that he fancied me, and I'd done my best to avoid encouraging his feelings. He'd proven himself to be intelligent beyond any white man I'd ever known. My parents had tried to persuade me, to no avail, to at least consider him as a husband. A husband and a family had been something I'd dreamed of since I was a little girl. At my age, most women were married. Though I didn't know my actual age, nor my birthdate, my parents guessed me to be five or so when they found me. And we'd celebrated the day I collided with my mother at the market as my official birthdate, which would make me twenty-five years old, or so.

"By the end of tomorrow, I'll have them back to you," I said, my skin heating under the tender gaze he bestowed on me.

"Good. They're for Friday's edition." He smiled and returned to his office.

"Saul would be a fine husband." Kipling perched on the corner of my desk, his mischievous dark eyes on mine.

My brow narrowed with an intentional warning. I glanced around for eavesdroppers before busying my hands with flipping through the papers. "Don't you pry into my affairs," I whispered. "You know I keep work professional, and Saul is a work colleague."

"There's no harm in falling in love with someone you work with." Kipling clasped his hand over his wrist and rested it on his thigh.

Isn't there? Annoyance surged in me, entirely aimed at *yours truly*. If I'd reined in the romanticized thoughts I'd allowed to flourish for Kipling Reed from the day he interviewed me for the position as his assistant, I wouldn't be distracted by something that could never be between us.

"You're one to speak on love. I've yet to see you court a woman." I pulled back my chair to put an extra few inches between us.

His lips parted in an easy smile. "I'm waiting for the right one."

The one you can't have.

The beautiful Willow Hendricks was a worthy candidate for the love of an honorable man like him. He was a gentleman who put the needs of others first and fought for the rights of the Negroes, poor, and immigrants alike. He possessed all the laudable traits I'd consider in a husband. A deliberation I'd had with my parents, and they'd promptly reminded me that Saul, too, possessed such remarkable characteristics.

Too many times, my mind had carried me away into a fantasy world of what it'd be like to be loved by Kipling. The endless hours we'd spent on the streets and in coffee houses gathering stories had only nourished the feelings of affection I held for him. We'd come back to the press and stay until darkness fell. Admittedly, it was improper for a woman to spend so much time alone with a gentleman.

Though I'd started out as his assistant, within the year he'd promoted me to a journalist. The male staff had bickered over my advancement, but Kipling had shut it down before it festered into needless awkwardness.

Often, when the nights became long, he'd signal a hansom cab to take me home. Each time he'd accompany me back, walk me to the door, and offer a friendly stroke of my shoulder or a kiss on my cheek, thanking me for my commitment to the paper. Oh, how desperately I wanted to tell him my dedication was not only to the newspaper but to him.

"Love is a tricky thing." I balled my fist in the folds of my skirt.

His playful laughter scalded my wounded soul. "What do you know of love?"

"Not much." I shrugged, refusing to meet his gaze and utterly unprepared for what he asked next.

"Have you ever been in love?" His words came out softer…thoughtful.

I elevated trusting eyes to his questioning ones. My tongue felt awkward and thick. "I–I have."

"And?"

"He didn't return my feelings."

"Well, it can't be Saul. I see how he looks at you," he said in a voice for my ears only. "Whoever the man is, he's a damn fool. Any man would be fortunate to win the heart of an exquisite woman like you." He shook his head with disdain.

I searched his face, yearning to find a glimmer of the emotions surging behind my breast, desperate to discover what I knew I'd never find. Instead, I recognized the respect and admiration he held for me. In that I suppose I should be happy, yet my chest tightened with displeasure and rejection.

"What?" His eyes widened in confusion.

"Nothing."

"But that sadness in your eyes. This man has obviously hurt you."

How could he not know I cared for him? Rage stewed in me at the daft man that sat before me with his mouth agape and his warm brown eyes roving over my face. His love for the chestnut Southern belle—with a heart so full of love for another man—hadn't dampened. I believed he'd put his feelings for Willow aside for the time being. For how long, I wasn't sure.

I'd come to believe Kipling would remain unwed forever. Maybe it was best that way. To see him with another woman…well, it was devastating to envision. My stomach grew heavy at the horrible selfishness of such a thought. *Don't I want him to find happiness?* Yes, of course I did.

"Let's not speak of personal matters." I pulled in my chair and lifted the quill from the inkwell. "If you'll kindly remove yourself from my desk, I've work to do."

"We *will* have this chat again and you'll tell me of the man who's too simple to see what he has passed up." He stood.

You! I screamed silently.

Infuriatingly…oblivious. My toes wiggled in my shoes, and I bit down hard on my tongue and muted the list of hurtful words I wanted to throw at him.

"We're meeting Frederick Douglass at noon to go over the injustice served by the city on the teacher."

Kipling casually walked to the front door, placed his silk top hat on his head, and slipped into his black frock coat. Then with a smile and a tip of his hat, he was gone.

Through the blur of my damp eyes, I stared at the delicate oversized snowflakes cascading like feathers from the sky and hitting the windowpane, only to melt and vanish into nothing, mimicking the hopeless love in my heart with the understanding that Kipling and I'd never be more than an absurd delusion.

I dropped my head, and the words on the parchment in front of me clouded in the well of tears threatening to wash the ink from the pages. If only I'd guarded my heart. I had no one to blame but myself, after all; I'd landed myself in this predicament to start with.

A woman of color married to a white man—why, it was inconceivable. I laughed out loud at my idiocy, then cringed as the unfeminine echo of my booming laugh lifted heads, stirring the loathing I'd held for a sound I couldn't control.

CHAPTER
Three

THAT NIGHT IN THE WARMTH IN FRONT OF THE FIREPLACE Mother and I sat in rockers, busying ourselves with rolling gray and brown wool into balls. Papa relaxed in a Louis-Philippe mahogany armchair, cushioned with green velvet, gifted to him by his sister. It was a grandiose piece he'd never have wasted money on, yet it had become *his* chair. He sat engrossed in the day's edition of the newspaper I'd brought him.

"Splendid paper," Papa said. "Young Kipling knows how to fill the pages with worthy articles that pique the interest of all people, unlike the twaddle the mercantile and political papers write aimed exclusively for the elite and social climbers."

"The same thing you say every night." Mother's gray eyes smiled at me over the top of her wire spectacles. Her gaze revealed the affection she held for my father.

"Kipling's delighted with your feedback on the paper," I said over my shoulder. "He won't let me leave without taking a copy for you."

The paper rustled as he turned another page. "And to think my girl has a hand in the stories he publishes," he said, his tone tinged with pride.

His love had been a constant in my life, and he remained my biggest advocator. Attending an all-black school had not given me a sense of kinship and had heightened my awareness that I was different. Though the children and I bore the same dark skin, my parents were white, and that made me stand out. And I became an easy quarry for the heartless jeering of my peers. The cruelest of my childhood ridiculers had been a boy. He'd planted the worry in my head that if my white parents fell on hard times, they'd sell me to the slave states for a tempting price; a fear that secured precedence in a tender child's mind. Their taunting had sent me running into my papa's arms.

"There, there. Don't cry, my little jewel. Tell me, what's your trouble," he'd said, his warm breath kissing the top of my head.

"Don't sell me."

"What rubbish do you speak?" He'd pulled me back and held me by the arms, his dark eyes confused and searching for answers.

I'd relayed to him what the boy had said. "I don't want to be different. I want to be like the other kids," I'd wailed with childlike understanding.

"You may always be different in the world's eyes, but it's what you believe inside that'll be your greatest friend or your enemy. Don't let others make you feel small and worth less than them because of the shade of your skin. Though you weren't made by us, the Almighty saw fit to give you to us, and each day I thank Him for allowing you to walk into our lives."

"Even if I'm not a boy?"

He'd gently swiped the tip of his finger across my nose. "Especially because you're not a boy."

I smiled at the memory. Many times throughout my life I'd come to him with my troubles, but I'd left the matters of the heart for my mother. However, I was sure she'd whispered my feelings for Kipling to him.

My thoughts turned to the previous night's dream, and an intense yearning lodged in my chest. My parents were creeping up on seventy, and life with them was beyond anything I could ever have imagined. They'd ensured that I never went without and had showered me with unconditional love. Despite the happiness of being their daughter, I could never calm the disquiet that had troubled me all my life—the longing for my real family.

"Mother…"

"What is it?"

"I had another dream last night," I said.

Behind me, Papa drew in a jagged breath. Guilt rushed through me. I didn't want to cause them pain. Why couldn't I be satisfied in all they had given me? They had risked so much. I knew the answer. It had always been clear—a part of me was missing, and no matter how I tried, I couldn't force the yearning from my heart.

"I heard you crying," she said, studying me keenly.

"They come almost nightly and change form slightly. Some nights it's the ship's hold, and other times there's the sound of howling dogs. I'm in a wooded area that resembles a swamp, and I'm being chased. But there's a woman holding my hand and urging me to run. The woman with the eyes I can't seem to forget. Then there's the man with skin like mine. He's gentle and kind, but I can never get a clear image of his face. He sings the same tune…" I began to hum the soothing melody running through my head. The tune with the lyrics lost to me.

"Maybe it's the longing to know where you come from that manifests in your dreams."

"If only I bore a brand or something, then maybe I could trace myself back to the man who owned me."

The word *master* would never part my lips. I was no man's property. I was Ruby Stewart, a free black woman. As a child, I'd taken my freedom, and no one would take that from me.

"The fact that you weren't branded has helped keep you safe this long." Mother's eyes implored me to let the past rest.

"I know." Sadness enveloped me.

"Can't you be happy for what you have here?" Her broad shoulders sagged, and she appeared weary and more fragile than usual.

"I am happy." My voice rose. "But each day I wake a part of me is missing. It's like a yearning that doesn't go away. A summoning." My hands paused rolling the wool, and I regarded her earnestly.

"A summoning of your heart," Papa said, rising. His shadow encompassed us. "You torment yourself, and that's the reason for the dreams." He tenderly squeezed my shoulder. "If I could give you the answers you seek, I would."

I covered his hand with mine. "I know, Papa." Tears sprang into my eyes.

"I fear you've become consumed with finding this man who may only be part of your imagination. And your heart has made you believe it's something more," Mother said.

Later that night in bed, I considered my parents' thoughts and questioned my reasoning and the push behind the visions and dreams that had come and gone over the course of my life. For a period I'd put them behind me, until Willow's alluring green eyes met mine. Eyes I'd seen before…I was sure of it.

CHAPTER
Four

THREE DAYS LATER I STEPPED OUT OF THE TENEMENT IN the Five Points after paying my respects to Mary and her family. Early that morning, she'd sent her eldest son to inform me of her daughter's passing during the night.

Grieving the loss of life, I wandered aimlessly down the alley, my mind preoccupied with how much Mary had suffered in her life: two stillborn births, her husband's death, and now her daughter. How much could a person handle?

Death in the Five Points was a daily occurrence; not only the murders but the mortality rate of children and infants was extremely high. Charles Dickens himself had written about the Points after his visit in '42.

Kipling strove to shine a light on the working class and the suffering in the Points through his newspaper as a way of giving the people a voice, unlike the dailies that were directed solely at the wealthy.

"Ah, look what we have here." A lewd voice jerked me from my pondering and sent my heart thrashing into my throat.

"Got ourselves a darkie," another man said.

They stepped out of the shadows ahead: one rangy and sky-high, the other thickset and mid-height.

"We'll fetch a hefty price for a well-kept darkie such as yourself." One dared to tip his hat, and his lips parted to reveal stained amber teeth.

I scanned my surroundings, frantically seeking an escape route while I glided my hand down the side of my skirt to the concealed pocket and removed my blade. "Stay away from me," I said with more grit than I felt inside.

"Or what?" They closed in.

"Or I'll drop you where you stand." I took a step forward, revealing my blade. The metal gleamed and made whizzing noises as I slashed it repetitively in midair, warning them to stand back.

Disbelief shadowed their faces, and they exchanged questioning looks. My heart leaped with anticipation. But they were quick to recover their composure.

The stocky one's laughter vibrated throughout the alley. "You think you can take the two of us?" He gestured between himself and his mate.

"Maybe not both, but one of you will take your last breath today." Fear bloomed in my chest and I sliced the knife maniacally at them.

They advanced. I dashed for the narrow gap between a dance hall and a boarding house. The hem of my dress caught on a plank and pulled me back so hard my neck burned from the snap. Frantically, I yanked the fabric from the board as the men darkened the entrance. Malicious grins spread across their faces.

"There's nowhere to run. You'll be a master's whore

before the end of the week." The shorter of the men crept forward.

I turned and fled, weaving around buildings and dashing down gaps, making my way to Cross Street. My lungs burned and my legs wobbled, feeling like they'd give out at any minute, as I swerved in the direction that would lead me out of the Points.

I cast a glance over my shoulder and stumbled over something in my path and went down hard. My tumble knocked the wind from me, and for a moment I sat stunned before becoming aware of a lumpy mass beneath me. I looked down and saw the body of a man lying stiff and cold on the frozen ground with a bullet in his chest. The pool of crimson that had oozed from him formed a solidified puddle. The man's death was yet another murder to add to the police's unsolved crimes of the Points.

My eyes darted to the men as they rounded the corner and looked up and down the street. Before their eyes fell on me and they sprinted toward me, I dug my heels into the ground, kicking at the corpse to get to my feet. Upright, I turned and ran. Taking a sharp left onto Mulberry Street, I dodged around crates, hecklers, and peddler's carts.

"A coin for a blind woman?" A beggar grabbed at the bottom of my dress.

I whipped my dress from her grasp. My mind screamed, *I'm sorry*, but my legs threw me forward. I darted down the alley in hopes of losing my pursuers as a fiery redhead stepped out on the stoop of a tavern and launched a bucket of filthy mop water into the alley. I came to a sudden halt, gasping as the water splattered over me, stinging my nostrils and dribbling down my face. The strong taste of lye soap and the grit of dirt ran over my tongue.

"I'm awful sorry, Miss Ruby," the tavern maid squeaked, horror widening her bright blue eyes.

I pulled myself from the shock of the mop water's assault and bolted up the steps and into the tavern. My heart thundered in my skull, blurring the girl's next words as I entered the poorly lit establishment and the stench of unwashed bodies, vomit, and alcohol curdled my stomach. I heard the footsteps of my pursuers as they raced into the alley and plastered myself against the wall inside the doorway. Closing my eyes, I tried to slow my breathing.

"You see a colored woman pass through here?" one of them asked the girl on the stoop.

"Sure did," she said.

My eyes flew open and fear tightened my chest. *No!*

"She went that way."

The sound of their heavy footfalls continued down the alley. I breathed a sigh of relief as they faded.

"What's she doing in here?" a blond bearded man of fifty years or so whispered to his companion.

Ignoring them, I strode into the back of the tavern to look for the owner.

"What's all the fuss?" Husky, dark-haired Joseph heaved a keg of beer onto his shoulder and turned. His thick black brows peaked in surprise. "Ruby, what are you doing here?"

"Slave traders tried to snatch me in the alley. I was on my way back from paying my respects to Mary Kelly." I held my side to ease the stitch and catch my breath.

"I heard she lost her girl." He pushed by me and disappeared through the door into the main room.

"Joseph." I chased after him. I'd interviewed the tavern owner for a story not long ago after his imports of whiskey were banned. And I'd helped in the delivery of two of his children.

He sat the keg down on the floor behind the bar. I moved in close to his side while eyeing the side door and the front, waiting for the men to stumble in.

He straightened, and his eyes dropped to my hand. "You best put that away."

I lowered my eyes and saw the blade I still clutched tightly. I felt for the secret pocket of my gingham dress and slipped it inside.

"How many times have I told you not to come to the Points alone?" he scolded in a brotherly manner.

"I consider myself street smart for the most part—"

"It has nothing to do with being street smart. There's always someone looking to make an extra coin. A black woman walking alone is an easy target here."

"I've learned to be aware of my surroundings no matter what neighborhood I visit."

"Do I have to sit here all day or are you going to waste my time talking to this darkie?" The same bearded man from earlier scraped back his chair and approached the counter.

Joseph filled a mug with ale.

"And one for my friend." The man kept his glassy light eyes pinned on me.

Joseph nodded and handed two mugs to the man. He

stumbled back to his chair and slammed the mugs down, sloshing ale over the tops that darkened the wooden table.

"I'll get my brother to take you wherever you are headed," Joseph said.

"Thank you."

"Now you best move into the back room until he comes for you." He tilted his head at the storage room.

In the back, I leaned against some crates to wait. I'd evaded capture today, but when would the next person looking to make some coin try to capture me? I heaved a somber sigh. "Free" was a funny word. A word the North used to appease the people that stood against slavery.

I'd spent a good share of my life helping runaways, and I'd listened to their stories and witnessed the horrors conducted on their bodies. I'd held mothers in my arms as they wept, grief overcoming them as they shared their memories of the children, husbands, and other family members their masters had sold off or killed. I listened as they told me of the punishments and rapes they'd endured. The men told me how they stood powerless while the master bedded their wife. Each story they'd shared, I'd never forgotten. Stories I refused to ignore unless I, too, became complacent to the suffering of my race. Across the nation, slaves cried out for a redeemer, and I wondered... had He forgotten them?

CHAPTER
Five

AFTER A QUICK STOP AT HOME TO CHANGE OUT OF MY dirty, wet clothes and wash up, I boarded a streetcar. I walked past the rows of seats with a sign that read *White Patrons Only*. Wiggling my way down the narrow aisle of white passengers, I stepped over their outstretched legs—they never obliged me by tucking in their feet. A pretty auburn-haired woman's face contorted with disgust. She leaned toward an older woman who bore the same upturned nose and whispered, her disapproving eyes never leaving me.

I narrowed my eyes at the ill-mannered women, squared my shoulders, and marched to the back of the car to the section labeled *Coloreds*. I dropped with a thud onto the hard wooden bench, but when I looked up to find the women watching me, I tilted my nose up. I owed the anger simmering in my chest to the dictatorship of this country—because they were responsible for putting an X on our chests, marking us as *nothings* by hanging despicable signs in public places. I wouldn't allow the women to see my displeasure over their whisperings and hostility.

A sharp ache thumped in my skull, and I massaged the tense muscles at the nape of my neck. *So goes my life,* I grumbled inwardly. I was exhausted and my day had barely begun.

Seated at my desk at the newspaper twenty minutes later, I mulled over the events of the morning.

I lived in a world where my kind was perceived as lower than even the immigrants the whites abhorred. My parents had drilled my worth as a human into my brain, and with that, the ostracizing of the nation I called home never calmed in me. It didn't make a difference if I lived in the North or the South; I'd still be viewed as lesser-than until the outlook of the men running this country saw the wrong in the monstrosities targeted against us and took a stand against the injustice.

For years the constant worry that my master would show up and take me back to work the fields or whatever job I'd be given kept me awake at night. At the docks three years ago, a group of sailors had almost taken my free-dom from me, but I'd fought them and wiggled from their grasp. I'd grown tired of being vulnerable, and after being robbed and attacked on my visits to the Points, I'd conjured up the idea of carrying a blade for protection. Secretly at first, I'd begun to sew the pockets in my clothing until my mother found out and questioned me. For the first time, I'd mentioned the attacks. Her motherly wings spread, and she forbade me from going alone again. But upon my in-sistence that people needed me, she'd brought the matter before my papa with the hopes that he'd put his foot down.

Though worry had permeated his face, he remained quiet for a dreadfully long time, until finally he spoke. "We can't accompany you every time you visit the Points. It may be best that you learn how to protect yourself."

Mother had started to speak, and he'd lifted a hand to silence her. "But you must be careful."

"Careful?" Mother had scoffed. "If someone ends up dead, folks would act first and think later. And if it were to go before the courts, she'd never stand a fair trial."

My thoughts returned to the present moment. I swallowed hard and whispered a grateful prayer that God had watched over me yet again.

"Ruby!" Kipling gave my shoulder a gentle shake.

"W-what?" I stared up at him.

His concerned dark eyes roved over my face. "I was in a meeting when you walked in, but I couldn't help but notice you were late. Are you all right? You appeared lost in a fog."

"I suppose I was. The morning hasn't been a pleasant one so far."

"I'm sorry to hear about Mrs. Kelly's daughter. But something tells me there's more." His tender tone soothed the tension of the morning but sent my heart to racing at an uncomfortable speed. Kipling could read me more than anyone.

"Slave traders..." I stood and moved away from the heat of his body so close to mine. I walked down the narrow hallway to the storage room to find a new ink bottle and paper.

"What?" He charged after me, his boots pounding the oak floors.

"Two men tried to grab me coming out of Mrs. Kelly's." I kept my back to him. Clearing my throat, I choked back tears.

"Ruby, did they hurt you?"

"No one will ever own me," I whispered through clenched teeth. "Not ever!"

Kipling's warm hands on my shoulders gripped my heart, and he gently turned me around to face him.

"Answer me. Did they harm you?" His fingers tipped up my chin, and bade me look at him.

I recalled the man's words: *"You'll be a master's whore before the end of the week."*

No man would use my body to pleasure himself without my permission. I'd end my life before I'd allow that to happen. After the Bloodhound Law—the Fugitive Slave act of 1850—was established, the capturing of others like me became a heightened concern for blacks and abolitionists alike. If Mother had her way, I'd be locked indoors, hidden from vigilant eyes. I couldn't live in fear—I wouldn't—but today had been too close. What if I hadn't moved swiftly and evaded the men set on capturing me?

A shudder ran through me. I mustn't think of it. I was safe, and in that, I counted my blessings.

"No, I surprised them by revealing my blade, and it gave me enough time to get the lead on them." Embarrassing tears rolled over my cheeks and tickled the curve of my neck before disappearing.

Kipling crushed me to his chest, and his arms swathed me in a protective cocoon, stealing my breath. In his desire to protect me, he'd forgotten himself. This exchange between a gentleman and a woman was hardly fitting for whites, but a woman of color—he risked bringing reproach upon himself and sending the hate mobs after my parents and me.

"You can't be going down there alone. I've told you before—"

"To take you with me." I finished his sentence and swiftly sidestepped out of his embrace. "I appreciate your concern but there are folks in the Points that count on me, and you aren't always available."

"No excuses. If something happened to you…I–I don't…" He swept his fingers through his dark locks.

"I'm not your responsibility. And you certainly can't be with me at every moment."

"But—"

"But nothing! Can you wait outside my townhouse for me to leave every day? Can you follow me to the market, the shops, the dock? No! Every day I walk outside I face the threat of being captured and thrown on a ship and smuggled off to a slave-owning state. It's just the way it is."

Kipling's hands slid down and captured his waist as he paced the small room. "Maybe we should lock you up until we leave for South Carolina," he said with a nervous laugh. "It'd make me feel better."

I crossed my arms and leveled a glare at him. "I'd like to see you try."

His lopsided grin summoned the usual fluttering in my stomach. "I take it that is a no?" he said with a laugh, his body relaxing.

"I'm glad you find amusement in my distress." I pretended to be irritated but felt my cheeks lifted into a smile.

It'd always been effortless between us until I ruined

everything by developing pesky feelings that jeopardized our friendship. We'd developed a bond I'd never risk by voicing my deeper affections.

"I do look forward to seeing Willow and Whitney again," I said.

"It's been too long..." Kipling's boyish grin slipped, and Willow claimed the space in his mind once more.

Sorrow weighted my shoulders, and I scurried past him into the hallway. I felt his eyes on me as I continued down the hall, and for a brief moment I allowed myself to imagine that the longing in his eyes spoke of his affections for me instead of my friend.

If only things were different; maybe in another time, or another world, he'd have returned my love.

CHAPTER

Six

L ATE ONE TUESDAY AFTERNOON, I RETURNED TO THE
newspaper after visiting the Old Brewery site that'd
been the focal point of the Five Points until it was
demolished last December. Kipling and I'd interviewed
Bishop Jones of the Methodist Episcopal Church about the
new mission being built on the lot.

At one time the Old Brewery had housed over one
thousand residents: beggars, prostitutes, pickpockets,
thieves, and murderers among them. The police dared not
enter the establishment without a large backup force. The
cellar of the building had contained twenty rooms and the
tenants often didn't see the light of day. One great room
on the main floor was named Den of Thieves. The horrors
that occurred in the place had been beyond imaginable.

"A letter came for you." Saul hovered over my desk
moments after I sat down.

I glanced up at him. "From whom?"

"The Hendricks woman again."

Excitement leaped into my chest. "Then don't hesi-
tate, give it to me." I held out a hand. He placed the letter in my palm, his fingers lingering a moment more than
necessary. Our eyes met, and I blushed at the affectionate

glimmer in his eyes. A flutter tickled my chest, but I stifled it and hastily rebuked him. "Watch yourself."

I shooed him away with a flick of my hand. He walked back to his office, his light chuckle trailing after him. Watching him, I admired the way he walked with confidence, and his broad shoulders. A woman would find solace and refuge in the shelter of his strong arms. "Get ahold of yourself," I whispered.

Tearing open the letter, I ran my eyes greedily over the first few words.

My dearest friend,

My heart swelled with warmth and I sank into my chair to devour each word.

I'm writing to ask your and Kipling's assistance in locating a slave child that I have reason to believe may have passed through New York. She was placed on the vessel Olivia I *in Charleston in '32, heading to New York.*

She would have been four to five years old when she escaped. Her given name was Mag. I know I'm grasping with so few facts, but if you could aid me in any way, I'd be forever in your debt.

I look forward to your upcoming visit.

Your friend,

Willow

I felt the color drain from my face, and a chill scurried up my spine. My heart reverberated in my skull. The letter dropped from my hand, bounced off the edge of the desk, and floated across the floor.

I couldn't think. Couldn't breathe. The murmurs in

the room drifted further away.

Mag…

Goose pimples swept over me.

There it was—the name that'd been in my mind for as long as I could recall. The name that echoed in the wind, in my dreams, and in the fleeting memories of an Irish boy. The one link to my past that I'd not spoken aloud since the day my parents claimed me as their own. They'd ensured I understood the danger of someone finding out my real name.

My lips parted and I softly spoke the forbidden name. "Mag."

My parents believed I was about the age of the girl Willow spoke of, but the chances of me being the girl were impossible—laughable, really. I blew out a long breath and squeezed my eyes closed.

Opening them after a few seconds, I stood and retrieved the letter. My hands trembled, and my body felt numb. Again I read the letter, studying each word with the desire to find a hidden code or some clue that'd reveal that the Mag Willow spoke of was me. Nothing showed itself in the letter. I read it again and again. Minutes passed before I pulled myself from my futile efforts. I folded the letter and tucked it in my top drawer.

The day passed slowly. When it came to an end and all the staff had left for the day and only Saul and I remained, I pushed back my chair and went to retrieve my coat and bonnet.

"You seemed to be distraught over the letter from your friend." Saul's silvery voice came from behind me.

I turned to him as he exited his office and placed his top hat on his head. His dark woolen overcoat lay over the crook of his arm. Saul wasn't overly handsome, but there was a gentle kindness about the man that calmed me.

"She gave me some distressing news." I wiggled into my winter cape.

"Do you want to talk about it?" he said.

I waltzed past him and strode to my desk. "No, I need time to absorb it, is all." I turned to find him buttoning his coat.

"The far-off look that paused your quill for most of the day wasn't enough?" In the dim light of the office lanterns, his beautiful coppery skin shimmered.

"Why are you watching me when you're supposed to be working?" I balled a hand on my hip.

"If Mr. Reed hadn't placed your desk outside of my office window, maybe I wouldn't find the view in here so pleasing." He thrust widespread arms toward the ceiling. A twinkle of amusement glimmered in his eyes.

What had gotten into the man? He was openly flirting with me. Heat flamed on my cheeks, and I busied my hands with tying the sapphire-blue silk ribbons of my bonnet.

"Blue has always been your color."

Ugh! I clucked my tongue. "Are you coming down with something?"

"What do you mean?" He looked at me, bewildered.

"Dare I say you're flirting with me, Mr. Abraham?" I said, my eyes never leaving his.

He shrugged nonchalantly. "Perhaps."

"I appreciate your friendship—"

His strong chin tilted up. "As I do yours. However, I'd prefer if you'd consider my standing proposal to court you, Miss Stewart."

Until now, he'd never been too ambitious with his intentions to court me. I regarded the man before me for a moment. He was chivalrous, made a decent wage, and had ethics comparable to my own. Yes, if I allowed myself to, I could fall in love with Saul. He'd been kind and patient. Saul carried himself with dignity; a proud man of color with a rare and admirable demeanor.

"After all these years? I thought you'd putter out and move on to another woman by now."

"That may have been so with another man. But I love you," he said.

Taken back by his bold confession, I lifted a hand to my burning cheek. "L-love me?" I repeated.

"I would go to your father tomorrow and ask for your hand in marriage, if you'd consider."

"I—I don't know what to say. I mean…I knew you cared…but love…I hadn't realized…"

"How could I not? I've watched you stumble in here exhausted each morning from your noble deeds in the Points. Without complaint you put in a full day's work, then race off to do Mr. Reed's bidding, regardless of your exhaustion."

At his insinuation of me chasing Kipling, I twisted away from him to hide my embarrassment. Was I that transparent? No, surely not. Panic tightened my chest.

"I know"—he'd come to stand behind me—"that you

leave for Charleston soon. I…" His words trailed off and he dropped his eyes.

Something in me needed to know what he intended to say. "Go on," I said without moving.

He inhaled a deep breath before I felt his hands grip my shoulders and turn me to face him.

"Saul…"

"Shh." He placed a finger to my lips. "Don't speak. I fear I'll lose the courage to say this if I don't say it now. I want you to be my wife. I know your heart yearns for another—"

"What—"

"Let me finish. What you desire can never be."

He knows about Kipling. My eyes darted back and forth, searching his. I didn't read judgment or harshness in his gaze, only the desire of a man.

"If you'd give me a chance, I'd love you with all that I am. Our life together could be beautiful. In time you may learn to love me." Sadness reflected in his eyes. "But if not, a life spent listening to your boisterous laughter and watching you mother our children would give me great pleasure. You're a woman deserving of love. It hurts to see you pine after someone that can never be yours."

He knew my deepest secret. Kipling had been too much a numbskull to see, but Saul had seen through me. The knowledge of this panicked me, yet washed me in relief at the same time.

"I don't know what to say." My body quivered under his hands. Strong yet tender hands. A tear crept out of the corner of my eye.

"Don't answer now. Go on this trip you've planned and when you return you can inform me of your decision." His large thumb stroked the tear cascading down my cheek before he stepped back.

I had no words to say. I nodded and lifted my fur muff from my desk and slipped my hands into it.

"Let me see you home."

Again, I nodded.

CHAPTER
Seven

THAT EVENING, WITH THE LETTER GRIPPED IN MY HAND, I entered the dining room to join my parents for supper. The glass oil lamps sitting in the center of the oak table bathed the room in a soft ambient glow and caught the gold embroidery in the burgundy curtains hanging from the room's two windows overlooking the street.

Mother had prepared a meal of light bread, fish, and stewed fruit.

"Good evening," I said, sweeping into the room.

"Ruby, my darling," Papa said, offering me his cheek for a kiss.

I pecked his weathered cheek and circled the table to plant one on my mother's before sliding into my appointed chair and tucking the letter under me.

"It looks lovely, Mother." I smiled at her.

Though Mother tried her best at cooking, her meals were barely palatable. Papa had afforded us the luxury of a hired cook. Martha, a freed black, arrived soon after my parents had decided to keep me. She had been with us until her daughter had died during childbirth—when I was twenty—and she needed to help her son-in-law care for their three children. I loved her dearly, and my monthly visits with her hardly satisfied the ache of missing her daily presence around the house.

"Did you forget my paper?" Papa asked, picking up his white cotton napkin and tucking it into the collar of his shirt. His thick silver brows arched.

"I'm sorry, Papa. Forgive me, but it slipped my mind."

"That's unlike you." Mother passed the platter of fish to Papa, her expression concerned.

"I suppose I got sidetracked. I was preparing to leave when Saul approached me—"

"And?" Mother said with suspicious enthusiasm.

I expelled a calming breath. "He offered me a proposal."

Mother exchanged a look with Papa, and I got the feeling they were aware of his intent to propose.

"But I'm guessing you anticipated him asking?"

"Yes," Papa said. "At his request, I met with him for dinner last week. He told me of his intention to ask you to enter into a courtship with him, and I gave him my blessing."

I stared at them, dumbfounded. They'd certainly been tight-lipped about the matter.

"Do not be upset, my dear. You must understand Papa's and my concern," Mother said.

"And what is that?"

"We are getting older," Papa said. "And we do not wish to see you left without anyone to care for you."

"I'm quite capable of caring for myself." I filled my glass with cordial and took a long sip.

"We're aware of your capabilities. But knowing you'll not be alone and would have a family of your own would ease much worry for your mother and me."

"He's a good man, and you should consider his proposal," Mother said.

"I know." I picked at the chip on the corner of my plate with my fingernail. "It's just…"

Papa's palm hit the table and Mother and I jumped. "It's time you shook the idea of Kipling from your mind and your heart."

Tears swarmed in my eyes, and I dabbed them away with the corner of my napkin. Rarely had I witnessed him lose his temper, and when it was on my account, it upset me. His approval meant everything to me; his disapproval was unthinkable.

He continued sternly, "That nonsense will give you a lifetime of heartache. Life's hard enough for you without these silly thoughts you entertain."

"You're right. I know you are. I promised Saul that I'd think about it and give him my answer upon my return from Charleston."

"Good." His voice softened.

"There's another matter I must speak to you about," I said.

Mother adjusted herself in her chair. "What's that?"

I removed the letter and placed it on the table. "I received a letter from Willow."

Mother's eyes lit up. "How's she faring?"

"Fine." I unfolded the letter and slid it across the table to her.

She eyed me curiously. Her lips moved silently as she read the letter.

"Oh, my!" she sighed, placing a frail hand to her chest. She handed the letter to Papa.

Mother and I sat unmoving. I held my breath as I watched him read it. The previous tautness on his face surfaced once more.

"Do you think the child could be me?" I asked.

He sat for a moment without speaking, his eyes scanning the letter again.

"You mustn't get your hopes up. It could simply be a coincidence," Mother said.

"But I can't deny the possibilities."

Papa folded the letter and handed to back to me.

"Please, Papa, what are you thinking?" I pleaded, reaching out to rest my hand on top of his where it lay palm down beside his plate.

"Unless Mag's merely a figment of your imagination, we believe it to be your real name. It was the one thing you were certain of when I found you. When you came to us, you were very traumatized; wetting the bed until you were well over ten. You wouldn't sleep in the dark, and we had to burn a lamp in your room all night for years. Sometimes, when a child goes through a lot at a young age, they create images in their minds."

"We've been over that," I said with determination. "Regardless of the dreams and visions, I've always been certain that Mag's my name. It's the one piece I hold that I haven't forgotten…the key to my past. I recall Will calling me by that name during our time together on the streets and on the ship. Somewhere along our journey I must have told him that was my name."

My stomach curdled with the memory of the rocking of the ship and how I had vomited for days until I thought my tummy would lurch from my mouth. Then came the hunger that had scorched and ripped at my insides, followed by weakness and the torment of hallucinations. At night in the pitch black, I cried for something or someone I didn't remember.

The day we landed in New York, we scurried off the ship before the crew unloaded the cargo. The bright sun was blinding and fear soon snatched at me as I beheld the smoke-laden sky. Buildings rose as tall as the clouds and the streets and docks were thick with people, who towered over me as they pushed and shoved their way through the press. Will had clasped his big hand over mine and led me away.

Then, in our pitiful makeshift shelter at night, he'd held me when the ground chilled as the evening temperatures dropped. His firm young body had spooned around mine, and he'd whispered words of comfort as the night terrors came.

"Ruby darling, you don't look well." Mother's soft hand covered mine, where it lay trembling on the table.

I shook my head and squeezed my eyes shut to cut off the threatening tears. "I'm fine."

Later that night, I opened the double doors leading out onto the balcony overlooking the streets below. Brownstone buildings spread out over the neighborhood for as far as one could see. Black metal gas lamps cast dark shadows in their soft amber glow spilling out over the snow-covered streets.

A carriage pulled up outside a townhouse, and a man stepped out and turned to offer a hand to someone inside. A bonnet poked out, and a woman clad in blue and white emerged. The gentleman clasped her hand in the crook of his arm, and their happy laughter wafted through the brisk evening air. He walked her up the steps to the front door, and with a quick glance around, he stole a sinfully romantic kiss from his lady.

My heart swelled with the desire to be cherished and loved like the vision in blue below. I crossed my arms over my white cotton nightgown and pulled my red knitted shawl snuggly around my shoulders, gazing up at the sky. Clouds stretched across it like draped sheer fabric, veiling the stars and giving the moon an uncanny, misty glow.

Often, I'd come out on the balcony and think on the man who haunted me before my thoughts would run to the imaginary family I'd made up in my head: a mama, a papa, and maybe a sibling or two. Did they think of me as I did them, or had I become a faded memory?

CHAPTER
Eight

TENSION KNOTTED MY NECK ALL MORNING, AND I RUBBED a hand over the nape of my neck to ease the ache. From behind the drapes in the parlor window that overlooked the front street, I watched Kipling exit the carriage. It was the morning of our departure for South Carolina.

I moved away from the window and ran a hand over my recently shorn hair. Together we'd decided that for our journey to Charleston I'd travel as Kipling's manservant and he'd become a planter from Virginia. Which wasn't too far-fetched, as Kipling was born and raised in Virginia, living there until he gave up his work in politics to aid in the abolitionist movement.

Early that morning, I'd bound my breasts before slipping into a loose-fitting boy's shirt, dark trousers, and an oversized coat.

Mother shuffled to her feet from the rosewood settee, knotting her lace handkerchief in her fingers. "Please be careful."

"This isn't my first time in disguise."

"But you've never gone this far South before. We've managed to keep your identity hidden. I'm worried—"

"Don't fret, Mother Dearest. All will be fine." I pulled the wooden buttons through the buttonholes of my coat and tugged at the hem. "How do I look?"

"Like a son instead of a daughter," she said with a nervous laugh.

"Perfect." I smiled broadly, feigning courage I didn't feel to relieve her anxiety.

"We shall miss you terribly." She lifted her handkerchief and blotted the corners of her eyes.

I gathered her into my arms and kissed her soft cheek, soaking in the whiff of jasmine—a familiar, comforting scent I associated with my mother. "I'll be back before you know it," I whispered.

The brass door knocker clanged as Kipling made his arrival known.

"Good morning, sir." I heard our butler say. "Miss Stewart's in the parlor. If you'll come this way."

Mother hugged me with great earnestness. "A promise is a promise, Ruby Stewart," she scolded affectionately.

Pulling back from her arms, I gazed into her tear-filled eyes. "I'll come back." I placed her hand over my heart, sealing my promise.

"You're a good girl. A treasure to your father and I in our old age," she said.

"Mr. Reed has arrived," the butler said from the doorway.

Kipling moved past the silver-haired man and walked into the room with his top hat in his hands. His friendly smile lit up the room, and he strode toward my mother with widespread arms. "Mrs. Stewart, as divine as ever," he almost sang.

She dismissed his genuine attempt at charming her with a wave of her hand. "Taking my girl away doesn't have you in my good books right now, Mr. Reed." Mother's thin lips pressed tight, but a glimmer of admiration for Kipling shone in her eyes. She'd always spoken highly of him.

"I can hardly go to Charleston without my top journalist. She's the life behind the newspaper, my secret weapon, per se. With her by my side, we're outselling our competition. And I owe it all to her—she can sniff out a story before it happens and brings an unbiased opinion and a fresh perspective."

I blushed with pride at his praise. "If we expect to make our train, we need to leave soon." I slid on the men's leather gloves to conceal my small, feminine hands, then picked up the brown felt hat from the settee and pulled it down over my ears.

"Mrs. Stewart, always a pleasure," Kipling said with a half bow.

"Take care of her." Mother's voice cracked as she gripped Kipling's hands and squeezed. "Bring her back safely. She's all we have."

"I assure you when she isn't with me, she'll be in good hands. Miss Hendricks isn't one to let those she cares for be put in harm's way." He spoke with grave seriousness, understanding my mother was entrusting him with me.

Tears clotted in the base of my throat.

"Someday I hope to meet this woman you both speak so highly about," Mother said.

"Perhaps, one day soon, she'll revisit New York. Like

her father before her, she has many ties with abolitionists, among others, in the North and in Canada." He spoke with deep, unbridled passion. Not from the love he held for Willow as a man, but with admiration for her mission to help slaves.

"Tell Papa I love him and I'm sorry I missed him this morning." I leaned in and kissed my mother's cheek one last time.

Kipling offered me his arm. "Shall we?"

"Must I always blend into the walls with you?" I said, agitation growing in me.

He frowned and gawked wide-eyed from Mother to me.

I huffed and crossed my arms.

"W-what did I do wrong?"

"Since when do you offer a man your arm?" I said.

"Oh!" Enlightenment crossed his face. "Of course; forgive me for my slipup."

"A slipup we can hardly afford." I stalked past him and out into the foyer.

"She's been a basket of nerves all morning. Please forgive her for her rudeness." Mother's voiced filtered out of the parlor.

"She's taking a great risk, going into the belly of the snake," Kipling replied.

"If someone suspects you two aren't who you say you are, Ruby could be taken. Please, I beg of you…" Mother's voice broke, and my throat thickened. "Protect her with your life."

"On my honor, I promise her well-being is my utmost

priority. No business matter or story is worth losing her. I love your daughter…"

Love? Could it be? My pulse raced.

"She's like a sister to me," he said.

He may as well have held my beating heart in his clenched fist as the pain of his words seared into my brain.

I picked up my satchel sitting by the door. The butler had seen to it that my trunk was loaded on the carriage. Opening the door, I exited the house, walked down the steps, and entered the carriage.

Kipling soon boarded and sat down across from me. He eyed me, leery. "Are we good?"

"Certainly," I said with a tilt of my nose.

He didn't deserve my contempt, but at the moment I didn't care. The freshness of his words and the stress of what lay ahead took precedence over all other thoughts of guilt and self-blame in my mind. I turned and looked out the window and not a word passed between us for the rest of the way to the station.

CHAPTER
Nine

As the steamboat pulled into Charleston Harbor, my nerves surged. The journey had been difficult and dangerous. So far, with Kipling's and my work with fugitives and the abolitionist movement, I'd never been required to travel into the Deep South. The deeper we'd gone, the higher my anxiety rose.

You're asking to get captured, I'd told myself countless times through the trip. The segregation of the blacks in the free states became a whole different matter, the farther South we went. In New York, like all blacks, I had an invisible label—*Freedom Limited*—slapped on my forehead. Since we'd boarded the steamboat for the rest of the journey to Charleston, I'd noticed how the blacks' heads hung lower and eye contact between a white and a colored was forbidden. They scurried to do their master's bidding, and for the most part evaporated into the background as though they were cargo.

I'd made the mistake of looking a woman—resembling a penguin with her robust stomach and beak-like nose—in the eye. Now as I stood beside Kipling at the railing, I lifted a hand to my cheek at the memory of the sting from her slap.

Overhead the sky rumbled with heavy-bellied clouds and cast a gloominess over the Charleston Harbor stretching out before us. Vessels crowded the harbor. Workers and supplies ready to be loaded onto ships congested the bridge. Citizens stood waiting for incoming passengers, filling the empty spaces on the pier with specks of vivid color.

My stomach rolled with the worry of what may or may not lie ahead. What information would Willow have on the slave child she mentioned in her letter? I peeked inside my pocketbook to make sure the letter hadn't disappeared.

"I assure you, whatever that pocketbook contains, it hasn't vanished since the last hundred times you've checked," Kipling said out of the corner of his mouth.

I heard confusion in his voice, and I feared Kipling thought I'd lost my mind. I'd decided against mentioning Willow's letter to him. Since the arrival of the letter, the puzzle in my mind and endless questions over my vague past had built a pile of hopeless dreams. Confiding in him over something that could be nothing but my wishful thinking was an embarrassment I preferred to avoid.

Later we stood before the Charleston harbormaster, and he held out his meaty hand. "Papers for the slave."

Kipling removed the forged documents claiming me as his slave from his pocketbook.

I hung back with my head bowed, holding our satchels. I prayed the harbormaster wouldn't notice my trembling.

Rightfully, I *was* a slave, and I'd hidden all my life in plain sight in New York. As the story went, I was the orphan daughter of my parents' cook, who died in the cholera outbreak of '32—the year I'd arrived in New York. And they couldn't bear to think of me being homeless and gave me room and board in exchange for helping them around the house.

Then they went as far as enrolling me in school, and they'd needed a last name—the cook hadn't taken one after her escape from slavery. That day I became Ruby Stewart.

One Sunday when I was seven, as my parents and I exited the house to attend morning service in the black community, a prune-faced neighbor had cornered us. "What are you doing letting that darkie live in your house? And dressing her up like she's a doll or something...why, I've never seen the likes of it." She'd clucked her tongue.

Papa tightened his grip on my hand, and his voice boomed. "We are doing the Lord's work. Who are you to question His work?" He acted as if he were more appalled at her than she was of him.

"The Lord's got no love for the devil's spawn." Her green eyes flashed like the devil's himself. "Look at her dark skin—it's the evil of the devil manifested. God's warning us of the evil that lies within them."

"If God allowed us a peek into your so-called Christian soul, we'd find a darkness darker than any Negro's skin," Papa said.

Taken aback by his rebuke, she snorted and stomped off with a quick "I'll pray for your soul" thrown over her shoulder.

"As I will yours," he whispered. His shoulders rose and fell.

"I'm sorry." I peered up at him.

His gentle, sad eyes looked down at me. "For what?"

"For making that lady not like you."

"It isn't me, nor is it you, she doesn't like. Somewhere in life, she's developed a prejudice that even she doesn't understand."

I snapped from my memory as the harbormaster asked, "What brings you to Charleston?"

"Here to help my sister's husband. He's taken a fall from his horse and needs help managing his plantation," Kipling said.

"Got no overseer?" The man's voice hitched.

I fought the urge to squirm in my ill-fitting boots.

Kipling adjusted his weight to his heels and arched back his shoulders. "He does. You see, they aren't rich folk and can only offer the man employment a few days a week. Surely you can understand the hardship of putting meat on the table."

"What makes you think I'd know?"

"A harbormaster can't make that good of coin, can he?"

Hiding in the shadow of the brim of my hat, I dared to sneak a peek at the man. His unfriendly gaze registered on Kipling.

"Times are hard." The man folded the papers and handed them back to Kipling. "Next," he said and waved a hand for us to move along.

Kipling's pace was swift and, with my desire to be out of sight, I chased close on his heels down the dock after him.

"I'll hire a carriage, and we'll be on our way to Livingston." Kipling tilted his head to look at the darkening skies.

By the time we left Charleston behind and the countryside came into view, the skies had let go.

Kipling regarded me, seated across from him. "The threat of discovery has passed. Yet your smile has not returned. Are you not happy to be seeing Willow and Whitney again?"

"Yes. Quite." I stopped picking at the edge of the windowpane with the tip of my gloved finger.

"Then why the solemn demeanor?"

I offered a bright smile for his sake, while the twisting in my stomach never eased. He smiled back at me before resting his head back against the seat and closing his eyes. Opening the pocketbook, I withdrew the letter. The list of what-ifs had toyed with me throughout the journey. The stationery had become crumpled and worn from the many times I'd read the letter, searching for what, I wasn't entirely sure. Hope? Maybe. Or something to grasp onto.

CHAPTER
Ten

WHEN WE PULLED INTO LIVINGSTON, KIPLING looked out the gap between the curtain and the window. The weariness from our journey faded as his expression transformed into one of wonder—a look he often wore when he thought or spoke of Willow. A pang seized my heart, and without looking, I knew who'd caught his attention.

The driver opened the door, and I could see Willow waiting on the front gallery. She stood shivering in her rain-drenched blue gown. Her pinned-up hair had flattened in the rain and escaped tendrils cascaded over her shoulders. Excitement and anticipation animated her face. I felt a twinge of jealousy. Only *she'd* be an image of beauty and poise in her given state.

The driver waited for Kipling to exit, but he sat unmoving as if lost in a trance, his expression tender. At that moment, I felt a strange connection between us—the respect and passion he held for Willow, a woman who viewed him as a friend, matched my affection for a man who'd become my greatest of friends.

"Sir," the driver said.

Kipling shook his head, and his eyes fell on me. Though

I wanted to offer him a friendly smile, I couldn't. The dread of having to watch Kipling swoon over Willow plunged me into despair. She didn't deserve my ill thoughts, nor did he, but I couldn't shake the despondency overshadowing me.

Kipling opened his mouth to speak, but then as if reconsidering, he stepped out.

The driver stood holding the umbrella over Kipling. I disembarked and closed the door. Kipling splashed through the puddles toward Willow and the shelter of the gallery. The driver ran to keep up with him, never once offering the courtesy of cover from the storm to a slave. I hastened my steps to follow behind my master…my friend.

After a stableman came and took the driver and horses around back, Willow spoke. "What happened? Where's Ruby?" Disappointment lined her words.

Guilt and shame swept over me at the jealousy I'd harbored over Kipling's feelings for her. She was my friend, and her affection for me was palpable in her voice.

"I give you Jacob." Kipling sidestepped to give Willow a clear view of me.

I removed my hat and bowed graciously.

"It's a pleasure," Willow said to me and eyed Kipling with building annoyance. "That's all well and good. Now, answer my question. Was she ill?"

Kipling tipped back his head and laughed. His amusement was utterly lost on her.

Mary Grace and a tall, lanky slave girl stepped out onto the gallery. Mary Grace's face radiated her delight at our arrival but soon slipped into the same puzzlement on Willow's face. The other slave girl stood with her hands aligned at her sides and her eyes fixed on the ground.

"Mary Grace, please see to it that our guest is fed and made comfortable until Kip's ready to leave," Willow said.

Mary Grace gestured for me to follow, and replacing my hat, I hurried after her.

"Sending me on my way already?" I heard Kipling say as we rounded the gallery to the back of the house.

I halted as I took in my first view of a working plantation. In New York, I was used to being the minority, but as I looked out over the grounds, I saw a sea of people with complexions like mine. A sense of kinship gripped me.

"Sir, follow me," Mary Grace called from the bottom of the steps.

I nodded.

She pivoted and made her way to a small outbuilding not far from the main house. I clambered down the steps after her, pulling up the collar of my coat to cut off the rain trickling down my neck. She waited for me to catch up before pushing open the door and climbing the couple of wooden steps and going inside. From the doorway, I realized it was a kitchen of sorts.

"Come on, get in here before the rain washes you away," she said.

I stepped inside and glanced around the room, inhaling the scent of lemon and lye soap. In the center of the table sat a blue, flower-patterned bowl filled with polished red apples. Shelves were lined with jars of spices, dried herbs, and various cooking ingredients. Each item was color-coordinated and facing straight outward.

Everything in the room had its place. I became aware of the rain dripping from my clothes and puddling on the recently mopped floor.

"Don't worry about the mess. It's nothing a quick mopping can't take care of," she said, avoiding my gaze. Her stiff posture suggested she was on edge at being alone with me.

"Mama doesn't take too kindly to folks messing around in her kitchen. If it's all right with you, I'll fix you up a small bite to hold the stomach cramps at bay until she makes her way down here."

In the corner of the spotless plank countertop, she removed a white cloth and revealed a loaf of bread. "Made fresh yesterday."

My mouth salivated and my stomach rumbled with spasmodic hunger.

She cut off a thick slice of the loaf, carved off a wedge of butter, and slathered a generous helping over the slab of bread.

I took a seat on one of the two chairs at either end of the wooden table. A bench sat on one side of the table. At my back, the open fire warmed my chilled bones.

"You don't talk much, do you," Mary Grace said without turning.

"For the part I had to play since we left home, it was easier to be quiet." I removed my hat.

Mary Grace spun with the knife in hand, her mouth agape.

I grinned, rubbing a self-conscious hand over my short-cropped hair.

"Ruby!" She dropped the knife, and it clattered on the floor.

"Shocking, right?" I laughed.

She shook her head.

"I could hardly travel alone with a white man. And we thought it best if I took on the alias of Jacob, the man-servant to Mr. Reed, for most of the journey."

A beautiful smile crept across her face. Captivating hardly seemed like the appropriate word to describe the beauty of Mary Grace. Her dark eyes were tinged with green, and her flawless caramel skin was smooth and silky, like freshly whipped butter. Her exotic appearance was dangerous for a mixed woman, and I'd remembered the price that beauty had cost her. My stomach hardened with the recollection of what she'd suffered.

She turned and grabbed a plate from the cupboard and brought it to me, setting it down on the table.

"It's good to see you again." I lifted the bread and, not waiting for a reply, sank my teeth into it. My eyes widened as the delectable taste of molasses in the oat bread and the creamy saltiness of the butter sent my taste buds into blissful happiness. I moaned with satisfaction and swallowed. "Who made this?"

"Mama." Pride shone on her face.

"Ah yes, I do recall Miss Willow singing the praises of your mama's cooking when you all were in New York."

"Mama says she doesn't know how Miss Willow remains slim with her love for food."

Born perfect, the demon in my ear chimed. *Stop it!* I gritted my teeth and lowered my eyes, ashamed at the sinful chirping in my head.

"Is something wrong?" Mary Grace's pride wilted into confusion.

"No," I said. "But if you don't mind, I'd love to be rid of these clothes and slip into something more feminine."

"Certainly; I'll have your luggage taken to the cabin. You can change before we head up to the main house to surprise Miss Willow and Miss Whitney. That's if Mr. Reed hasn't given it away already."

"Very much appreciated." I stuffed the last of the bread in my mouth and brushed the crumbs from my lips with the back of my hand.

"Yes, manly indeed," she said with a giggle, her eyes sweeping over me from tip of my oversized boots to the top of my wooly mane.

CHAPTER
Eleven

MARY GRACE SHOWED ME TO A CABIN THAT SAT APART from the others in the quarters, tucked in the shade of two massive live oaks, and positioned to overlook the river. Red and pink camellias lined the stone walkway leading up to the front porch. Their delicate bonnets tucked in, shielding them from the pelting rain.

"Welcome to the marriage cabin." Mary Grace's eyes gleamed with amusement as she pushed open the door and motioned for me to enter.

I stepped inside, arching a brow at her reference. "Marriage cabin?"

The one-room cabin smelled of the same lemon and lye soap as the kitchen building. On the small table sat a vase of fresh flowers and against the wall to the left was a bed covered in a patchwork coverlet. Next to the bed stood a walnut vanity with a mirror. Yellow gingham curtains hung from the single window by the door.

"Mr. Hendricks had it built after he agreed to let Gray and I get married. Since then, when husbands and wives visit from other plantations, they request the use of the cabin for some alone time."

I squirmed as it dawned on me that she was speaking of the lovemaking between a husband and a wife. "I would've been fine with bunking in one of the other cabins."

"Miss Willow would have none of that. It's bothered her something awful to make you stay in the quarters instead of putting you up in the big house. This cabin's the next best accommodations on the property, excluding the guesthouse, of course. Miss Willow wanted everything to be just so for your arrival. She about worked her fingers raw to make sure this cabin was suitable for you." Mary Grace rushed on as if she needed to defend Willow's honor.

On our previous meeting at the café in New York, I'd witnessed the absolute devotion she possessed for her mistress and Willow's high regard for her. Their sisterly bond and love signified an unnatural connection between a white woman and her handmaid. Assuredly, a danger for them both.

How Willow managed to run Livingston and devote her time to the Underground Railroad and not have keeled over in exhaustion was beyond me.

"She needed not worry about such things. New York may be a free state, but if you recall, segregation is very much alive. For the sake of Willow's *cause* and all, she can't afford to draw attention to Livingston, or herself."

Mary Grace's bosom rose and fell with relief. "She'll be happy to see you understand. Miss Whitney tried to convince her that you would, but you know Miss Willow when she has her mind made up—that's it." Her laugh was light and charming, whereas mine emerged like clapping thunder. "However, regardless of all that, we've waited with eager anticipation for your arrival."

"As have I."

She helped me slip into a peach-colored skirt and an ivory blouse. I ran my hands over the skirt, trying to smooth out some of the wrinkles. "It'll have to do."

"No one will notice," she said. "They'll be so happy you're here that a few wrinkles will be the last thing they care about."

I clasped her wrist and smiled, and moved to the vanity.

"The vanity used to belong to Miss Willow's mama. She had it brought down from the big house just for you."

In awe, I ran my hand over the exquisite piece of furniture. Love swelled in my heart for my friend and her efforts to make my stay as pleasant as possible.

I sat down on the stool and peered into the looking glass. Gliding a hand over my hair, I tried to tame the unruly ball of fuzz capping my head. The dirt-smudged face of the lad staring back at me wiped out any self-confidence I may have earlier possessed.

As if sensing my displeasure at my appearance, she said, "I know just the trick to fix your hair. I'll be right back." She turned, pulled her shawl up over her head, and hurried out into the downpour, closing the door behind her.

Soon she returned with an ivory piece of cloth. "This cloth is spun right here at Livingston. If it's all right with you, we could make you a head rag like mine." Uncertainty wavered in her eyes.

Around her full head of hair, she wore a cornflower blue cloth. I recalled the smoother, glossy appearance of her hair and how I'd marveled over it when she'd visited the café with Willow and Whitney. She'd worn it pinned up with a center part like all the fashionable ladies were wearing. It was a shame to hide hair like hers. Before I'd cut my hair, it'd scarcely been shoulder-length with a wooly texture. Beside her, I felt small and insignificant.

"I'd be grateful. Would you help me?"

She spun me around and swiftly her fingers went to work at concealing my hair beneath the cloth.

"Take a look." A pleased smile lifted her cheeks.

I peered in the mirror, and my hand fluttered to my chest. The tightly wrapped head rag showcased my high forehead and my mahogany complexion. My spirit lifted, and I turned to her and pulled her into an embrace. "I can't thank you enough."

"If you have a shawl in your trunk, I suggest you retrieve it, and we'll be on our way."

Minutes later, under the poor shelter our shawls provided, we raced for the house.

CHAPTER
Twelve

E NTERING THROUGH THE BACK DOOR, I FOLLOWED HER down a corridor that led to the front of the house. Excited voices carried from somewhere in the home.

Mary Grace paused outside the room the voices floated out from, and whispered, "I'll see you later." Then she sauntered off.

Left standing in the corridor, I eavesdropped on the conversation within. The happy chatter of children mixed with the gleeful voices of Willow and Whitney and a man's I didn't recognize. I heard Kipling's merry voice as well.

A servant with a rag and a bucket of water passed me in the hallway. She eyed me with curiosity before inclining her head. "Good day, miss."

I nodded and stared after her, wondering if her curiosity stemmed from my eavesdropping on her masters or from something else. Did she recognize me? Surely that was impossible, wasn't it?

Ruby Stewart, you've lost your mind! I could hear Papa say.

I raised a hand and rubbed the weariness from my eyes.

Taking a deep breath, I made my entrance. "Kipling has been talking like a lovestruck woman about this trip for months. Nothing would stop him from coming."

All eyes in the room turned to me. Their delighted expressions at my arrival were not mixed with surprise, and I guessed Kipling had informed them that I'd come after all.

Kipling's neck above his collar reddened, and a grin broke across his face. "Now don't be telling Willow stories of my affections when she's already spoken for."

I swallowed hard at his bold words. The bond he shared with Willow was profound, yet as complex as his and mine. The sooner I put my feelings to rest for Kipling, the better it was for all of us. Determination hardened in me to consciously dissolve the absurd sentiments once and for all. For the sake of our friendship I held so dear, I had to find a way to move past them. The image of a dark, smiling man with kind eyes sprang into my head, and I quickly pushed Saul Abraham from my mind.

Willow plucked me from my thoughts. "I'm so happy you came." She crossed the room and gathered me in a hug.

The mess of thoughts in my head caused my body to stiffen in her embrace. I peered at Whitney over her shoulder, where she stood with her hands tucked in front of her, smiling.

Willow pulled back, confusion in her eyes.

Whitney strode toward me. "We're pleased to have you," she said, patting my arm.

"Children, please go play," Willow said to Whitney's twin siblings.

I looked at the blond girl and dark-haired boy. They'd grown since I'd seen them last.

"Yes, Miss Willow," they chimed, and dashed from the room.

"Ruby, if you'll follow me," Willow said.

We passed Mary Grace in the corridor. "I intend to hold the child you were carrying when you were in New York." I told her.

Mary Grace beamed and nodded her head with enthusiasm.

Willow turned to me and took my hand in hers. Her forehead creased with worry. "There's something I must speak to you about."

I glanced past her to a servant as he walked by. And for a moment, I wondered what my life would have been like if I'd been a slave.

Willow murmured something I didn't fully catch, and I mumbled a thoughtless reply as I took in my surroundings. Her chatter continued, and I heard myself offer an incoherent response as a male servant polishing the spiral staircase captured my attention.

"Have I done something to displease you?" Willow waved a hand in front of my face.

I pulled from my daze and became confused by her question. "What? No."

"You seem disconnected or upset," she said.

"It's just...it's..."

"What is it?" She touched my arm.

"Is there a place we can speak in private?"

"Certainly." She led me down the mahogany-paneled

corridor to a closed door.

Whitney's footsteps echoed behind us.

Willow opened the door and gestured for me to enter. I moved hesitantly inside.

A portrait of a woman hanging over the marble-faced fireplace halted my steps. *No! It couldn't be.* My heart beat faster. But the eyes. The dark hair. It was her! She was the woman who inhabited my dreams.

Someone collided with me from behind, followed by another, and I stumbled forward from the impact, my eyes never leaving the portrait.

"What in the name of—" Whitney said in exasperation.

"The woman in the picture, who is she?" I said, regaining my balance.

"My mother." Willow stepped past me into the room. She smiled proudly as she turned to look at me. Her smile slipped. "Is something wrong?"

"Your mother…" My voice fractured, and I regarded the woman in the painting with intrigue, willing her to speak and answer all the questions ruminating in my mind.

Could Willow's mother be the woman? Had meeting Willow stirred up memories I'd learned to suppress? The resemblance between the pair was remarkable. Eerie, in fact.

"Olivia was her name." Willow's tone was soft, and her eyes focused on the painting.

"Olivia…" I rolled the name over my tongue. The likelihood that I could be the child Willow wrote about mounted—sending a shudder through me.

It was her! It had to be.

"You're frightening me," Willow said.

"I know her."

"That's impossible," she sputtered.

"I assure you it's not."

"What Willow's trying to say is her mother's dead. But you knew this already?" Whitney's brow narrowed.

I turned to look at them. "Forgive me. I didn't mean to confuse you." Nausea tugged at my stomach, and the room turned rapidly like the spinning top I'd played with as a child. I gripped the edge of the desk to steady myself.

Whitney took me by the elbow and guided me to a chair. "Sit," she ordered, and to Willow, "you too. You look ready to faint."

Willow shuffled to a chair next to me and took a seat.

"That's the woman," I said, "the one in my visions. Her eyes are...your eyes." I swung my head back to the portrait, then back to Willow. "As sure as I'm here now, she's indeed the woman. When I received your letter, I'd dared hope, but the impossibility of it all gave me cause to doubt."

"Stop." Willow held up a hand. "You're talking in riddles. What are you saying?"

I paused to gather the right words to say. Not hours ago I'd clung to a hope which had seemed as impossible as waking to find that a black president had succeeded President Fillmore instead of Franklin Pierce, who Papa was sure would be the fourteenth president of the United States.

My voice thick with emotion, I spoke. "I believe...I believe I'm Mag."

Willow's face drained of color, and her eyes lost focus.

"Willow!" Whitney snapped her fingers in front of her face before going to shut the study door.

Willow shook her head and rubbed her hands over her face and pulled them down, fixing her piercing green eyes on me—her mother's eyes. Certainty straightened my shoulders, Olivia *was* the woman.

"What makes you think you're the Mag I mentioned in the letter?" Her voice trembled.

"I remember the ship. I remember landing in New York. And I remember the name Mag. I wasn't sure if it was my name or someone from my past. But like a whisper in the wind, it's always been there in my head."

Tears flooded her eyes and rushed down her cheeks.

"Since seeing you in New York the dreams and visions have plagued me yet again. The desire to know where I've come from was rekindled. I need to know more. What do you know of this Mag you wrote about?"

She started slowly. "My mother found the child hiding on the plantation. She'd escaped the slave traders. They'd hidden in the swamps until Mother thought it was safe. Then they doubled back, and Ben disguised the child as a boy and put her on a ship to New York. You see, we don't even know if Mag reached New York."

"Why are you so insistent on finding this child?" I asked.

"Because…because I believe her to be the child of someone very dear to me."

I sat up straighter. "W-who is this person?" I swallowed the thickening in my throat.

"His name's Jimmy. He's a blacksmith here at Livingston."

"James," Whitney corrected. "His given name's James. His wife's name was Nellie."

"Do you recognize the names?" Willow asked.

I heaved a sigh. "No, I'd hoped...I..."

"We all did." Her shoulders slumped.

"Perhaps I can meet your blacksmith."

"No!" she gasped. Her eyes flew to me. My jaw dropped at her outburst. She hurried to explain. "When I told Jimmy about the name in the ledger and Ben revealed the details of the child, Jimmy was distraught. Told me never to speak of her again."

"Yet you continue to search for her?"

"Yes."

"But why?"

"Because I can't give up. If you could only see the ache in his eyes. Losing her broke him."

"You care for the blacksmith."

"Like a father," she said, barely above a whisper. Her shoulders slumped as if bearing an excessive burden. She swallowed back tears and looked at me, her eyes hollowed and troubled.

"He must be quite a man, to bring on such feelings," I said.

"He's extraordinary. Smart. Intelligent. Good at whatever he puts his hands to. He's been there for me through many dark times in my life. Guided me...and, I like to believe...loved me," she said softly.

It was apparent she held great affection for the

blacksmith and felt the need to protect him, which endeared her to me even more. "Will you introduce me to this man?"

Her eyelids fluttered with nervousness. "If you promise not to mention my letter. We must also be certain you're Mag. I can't risk breaking his heart again."

"Understood."

"Very well, then. Let us show you to your quarters." Willow strode toward the door.

"Mary Grace had my trunk taken to the cabin," I said.

Willow swung back. Worry permeated her face. "I hope you don't—"

I lifted a hand to stop her. "I do not take offense to staying in the quarters. The cabin's lovely. Besides, it'll be refreshing to be around others like me."

"See, I told you she'd understand." Whitney tossed an auburn ringlet over her shoulder with a satisfied look.

Willow's shoulders relaxed. "I'm sure they will be happy to teach you whatever you like. I do wish things were different. However, I appreciate your understanding."

"Of course." I followed her from the room.

"This Ben you mentioned, who's he?" I asked as we made our way back down the corridor.

Willow stopped in her tracks and turned. "Oh, for heaven's sake. I guess in all the excitement I forgot to introduce you. Come, I'll do that now."

Kipling and the other man were engaged in a conversation about politics. They rose when we entered. I studied the attractive blond man, who appeared to be in his forties. His eyes fell on Willow, and a rush of tenderness stole across his face. He regarded her the way Papa had me, with the desire to protect and an unrestricted appreciation for her as a woman, not marred by the views men often ascribed to women.

She walked over to him and patted his arm, smiling up at him with the same affection he bestowed on her. "Uncle, I'd like you to meet my friend Ruby. Ruby, this is Ben Hendricks."

He strode forward with an outstretched hand. "It's a pleasure."

His hand was warm and firm, his eyes kind and inviting, and I instantly liked the man. "The honor is mine, sir," I said, searching his face for a glimpse of a memory, but I came up blank.

"Do you recognize him?" Willow said.

Ben twisted to look at her, his brows knitted in confusion.

Hopelessness enveloped me. "No."

"She met him moments ago; of course she recognizes him." Kipling glanced from me to Whitney and then Willow, his confusion mirroring Mr. Hendricks's.

Willow looked to me. "Is it all right with you if I tell them what you told us?"

I nodded. Willow related to the men what we'd discussed in the study.

"What!" Kipling's mouth unhinged. "But you never said anything—"

"Because until now it seemed a far-fetched hope. Even after receiving the letter, I'd believed it was hopeless until I saw the painting. Then I hoped by seeing Mr. Hendricks he'd stir a memory, but I'm afraid I don't remember you," I said to Mr. Hendricks. Genuine sadness reflected in his eyes.

For weeks I'd clutched a thread of hope that maybe I'd finally have the answers I sought. That coming to Livingston would ease the ache of the unknown, but the answers had died with Olivia Hendricks and in my failure to recognize Willow's uncle. But what of the other man Willow had mentioned? Could I be his daughter? A small flame kindled in me.

"The blacksmith—when can I meet him?" My voice squeaked.

Mr. Hendricks drew in a sharp breath, and his eyes met Willow's.

"Soon, I promise," she said. "We need to approach this with the uttermost respect and care. I know it's wrong of me to ask, but I beg you for a little more time. We need to be certain."

"I'll respect your wishes. I do not want to cause him any unnecessary pain."

CHAPTER
Thirteen

THE NEXT MORNING, I STEPPED OUT ONTO THE STOOP OF the cabin. The grayness of yesterday had faded away, and the sun sat bold and proud in the vast blue sky. I took in the grand expanse of Livingston Plantation before my eyes settled on the pesky rooster perched on a fence post a shoe's throw away. He cocked his head and studied me with one beady eye.

I set my jaw and stared into that beady eye. "So, you're the one making all the racket."

He adjusted himself on the post and turned his body from me as if I was the one disrupting his morning.

"Good morning." Willow, all smiles, strode across the yard toward me with Whitney's little sister, Kimie, in tow.

The girl's advancement resembled more of a skip than a walk, billowing her green-printed calico dress. The morning sun gleamed off her blond hair arranged in a simple braid over her shoulder.

"Did you sleep well?" Kimie asked, her cheeks rosy from the early morning temperatures.

"Yes, until my little friend here decided it was time I rolled out of bed." I nodded at the rooster.

Willow laughed.

"Oh, that's Burt. He's ornery, but he's the best rooster we have on the plantation," Kimie said, hurrying to catch her breath before continuing. "Miss Willow says you help nurse the sick folks in the Five Points. And that I can show you around the quarters if you want."

I smiled at her. "I'd like that."

Her young shoulders arched back, and I noticed the budding of tiny breasts through the bodice of her dress.

"But first, I thought we'd show you around the grounds." Willow draped an arm around her shoulders. "Whitney wanted to join us, but she previously promised Mrs. Sterling she'd help with the delivery of her grandbaby when the time came. Mr. Sterling came calling this morning."

We strolled the grounds of Livingston, and soon I became lost in its beauty and tranquility. Gardeners had trimmed every shrub and tree with precise care. Dormant rose bushes showcased the front walkway to the main house. We turned down a pathway that led around a pond on one side of the house, past a small family graveyard enclosed in a white wooden fence. My feet paused as a headstone caught my attention; it sat farther back in the family plot and flowers had recently been laid, yet the earth around it appeared undisturbed. The gravestone read: *Katherine Shaw—1813–1835—Forever Loved.*

"Kimie, run along, we'll meet you in the quarters," Willow said.

After she ran off, Willow rested her hands on the fence, her eyes drawn to the grave. She heaved a sigh and gave me a sideways glance. "I...I..." She turned and I noticed how she chewed on the corner of her mouth.

"Willow, what is it?" I touched her hand.

Her eyes dropped to our fingers, lightly intertwined. She looked at me, her eyes hollow. "That grave belongs to my mother."

I frowned. "But it says Katherine."

"Come, let's sit." She guided me to a stone bench under a budding magnolia tree. Once seated, she said, "I've been told that after my father found her body, he buried her here without a headstone. In later years, troubled by her unmarked grave, he came up with the idea to use her middle name." She went on to explain about her mother's murder and the reason her father believed it necessary to cover up her death.

I sat in awe. Willow fumbled with her hands resting in her lap. A tear trailed over her cheek and disappeared. Her pain and longing were so familiar to mine. We both yearned for someone we didn't know.

"You go to great care to honor her still."

"The flowers?" She shifted to look at the grave. "No, that's Ben's doing."

"Oh," I said. "You're blessed to have an uncle that cares as much as he seems to."

"He's not truly my uncle," she said, her eyes pulling away from the grave. She looked at me as if she wanted to say something.

"He's not? But I thought you'd said—"

She released a long breath and told me the tragic love story of her parents. When she finished, her shoulders sagged as if she'd released a hefty burden, while my head whirled with bewilderment and admiration for the man whose character outstood anything I'd ever heard: his self-lessness and the profound love he'd carried for Olivia and Willow, giving them up so that they had a chance at a better life. The beauty in love such as his was something I strove to earn in my life.

My heart ached for my friend, who was drowning in the secrets she'd no choice but to keep. And for the first time, I noticed the tiredness in her eyes and how the girl I'd first met now lacked the beautiful smile of her former self. Weariness clung to her shoulders as though a yoke hung around her neck. I sent a prayer up to heaven that God would grant her the happiness she so richly deserved.

Soon, we made our way back to the main house. On the front gallery, we found Mary Grace's mama—Henrietta—sweeping leaves. Her deep voice rumbled from low in her belly as she sang the song "Amazing Grace," written by the former slave trader, John Newton. The richness of her contralto voice cloaked me in chills.

"Are you feeling better?" Willow called as we mounted the steps.

Caught up in spirit of song, the woman jumped and spun around. "Lard sakes, gal! No need to shout. I ain't but a hare's hop away." Her tone sounded gruff, but I noticed that look—the one Mr. Hendricks held for Willow. One of eternal love.

Her keen eyes roved over me. "Miss Willow speaks of your good deeds in de North. Takes a woman wid great courage to take on a country bound on wiping our noses in de dirt."

Astounded at her forwardness, I recalled the slaves on our journey and how they'd differed from her, so docile and resigned to the life placed on them.

"Some days I lack the courage I need." I spoke honestly, matching her directness. "I desire to see slavery end and will join others in the fight to secure equality for all mankind, no matter their situation."

"I see why Miss Willow's drawn to ya." Her laughter rocked the thickness of her waist. "She got dat burnin' in her eyes, too."

An affectionate smile etched Willow's face. "I'm going to show Ruby around the rest of the property, and then I'll bring her by the kitchen house for breakfast."

"I'll be heading dat way right away. I'll whip you up somepin', Miss Ruby, dat'll be sho' to stick to dose skinny bones of yours. How do you survive dose New York winters widout any meat on your bones?"

I belted out a laugh that ended in an unbecoming snort. Henrietta's lips twitched with a grin she kept at bay, but her eyes smiled. Deep creases etched her forehead and the corners of her eyes and jowls from sorrows I couldn't begin to understand, yet the warmth in her dark eyes captivated me. My thoughts turned to my birth mother, and I envisioned her being something like this woman.

"I survive with many layers," I said.

Henrietta sobered, and her mirth vanished. "Me too," she said and turned to walk inside the house, whispering over her shoulder a mumbled goodbye.

Had I said something wrong? My chest tightened as the door closed behind her. I looked to Willow, who stood gaping after her, confusion and concern wrinkling her brow. She turned to me, her lips parted, and a soft peep escaped her before she said, "I'm sure Kimie's wondering where we are."

We circled the gallery to the backyard, and crossed the work yard to the quarters. Burdened by what I'd done to offend Henrietta and the desire to make it right, I said, "Clearly I said something to upset her."

"I don't know what, but sometimes it's like little things will stir feelings or memories in her, and she goes to a dark place in her mind. Please don't worry; it'll pass," she said, as if she'd experienced the situation before.

I nodded, but it didn't alleviate the anguish I felt over offending her. Willow forced a tight smile as she tried to shuffle her own concern.

"Miss Willow, Miss Ruby." Kimie raced toward us. "Are you ready?" Without waiting for an answer, she clasped my hand in hers and pulled me forward.

Her excited chatter as she introduced me to people lifted my spirit and drew my thoughts away from what had transpired minutes ago. We walked up and down the wide pathways between the rows of cabins. At the back of each cabin, a small section was fenced off and housed a hog or two and chickens. Planted alongside the buildings were secluded gardens with new sprouts poking up out of the earth. Women boiled clothing in large iron pots over open fires. Children darted in and out as they worked. A grandmother with an unlit pipe clutched between her teeth squatted on the stoop of a cabin, holding a wailing child I recognized to be Mary Grace's daughter Evie.

"Morning, Sara." Willow waved.

The woman squinted in our direction, and as we drew closer, I saw cataracts glazed the woman's eyes. "It's a blessed day."

"Sara is Miss Willow's handmaiden's mama." Kimie hurried to spit out the mouthful of words, her young shoulders drawing back with pride. "Her and Esther minds all the small children. Most of the children call her Grannie because she spoils them with stories and loves on them."

"You be sho' to come back dis way today. I've fixed dat doll you brought by," Sara said.

A blush seeped over Kimie's cheeks. "Thank you." As we moved on, she said, "I don't play with the doll. It's just special to me, 'cause when I first came here after my pa burned in the fire, Mammy made it for me. She said it would watch over me while I slept and keep the bad dreams away."

"I understand," I said. She seemed satisfied with my response, and we continued with her tour of the quarters. She explained the tasks of each person we met and related several names of people that lived in cabins we passed. Her insight into their lives and the passion flowing from her led me to believe she spent most of her time here.

At a cabin a few doors down, Willow climbed the steps and called out, "Rose."

The door opened, and a middle-aged woman wearing a red head rag with wisps of gray hair escaping at the hairline stepped out wiping her hands on her apron. "You again," she said, looking at Kimie.

"How is he today?" Willow asked.

"Masa Hendricks jus' left from checking on him. Says

de foot should be fine to walk on in a few days."

"Can we see him for a minute?" Kimie craned her neck to see inside the cabin.

The woman smiled reverently at the child. "He'd lak dat, Miss Kimie. A purty nurse lak you would heal a heap of ailments in de boy."

Kimie grinned and slipped past her into the cabin. The woman stood back and gestured us inside. The toasty warmth of the fire in the room swept the chill of outside away. In a rocker by the fire sat a young boy who appeared to be twelve years or so. His bandaged foot rested on a crate and against the box rested a cane. One look at his other leg told me the walking cane was a frequent companion for the boy, regardless of the new injury.

Kimie was at his side. She lifted a gentle hand to his forehead. "You don't have a fever."

"Gal, I don't got de flu, I twisted my foot." He narrowed his dark eyes and brushed her hand away. "You don't need to be comin' down here evvy day fussing 'bout me."

"Parker, you be nice to Miss Kimie. She jus' showing you some love," the woman said.

"No use showing me no love, I won't be 'round much longer. I'll be off sailing before ya know it—ain't dat right, Miss Willow."

Willow stifled a smile and cleared her throat. "That's what we're aiming for."

The boy tilted his chin. "You see dere, Miss Kimie, I ain't going to be 'round much longer. I'll be a man on Miss Willow's ships, helpin' Captain Gillies manage de crew." He lowered his injured leg to the floor.

"Not if you don't rest that leg." Kimie bent and placed his leg back on the crate. "You'll find yourself with two bad legs, and Miss Willow won't be sending you on any ship. You'll be staying here and helping your papa."

Something told me she wouldn't mind that so much.

Parker huffed and gave her a scowl, but a gleam in his eye told me he cared for the girl more than he was letting on and maybe even part of him enjoyed her attention.

Leaving the cabin, we pushed on. Kimie stopped beside a woman who was bent over in a coughing spell. She rubbed her back and spoke soothing words to her, promising to come back with some of Mary Grace's "miracle potions"— that were sure to fix her right up.

"That girl has nursing in her blood," I said.

Willow regarded the girl with fondness. "Yes, we believe so. When Ben makes his rounds to check on the ailing, Kimie's usually at his side."

"I could use someone like her in the Points."

"She's a light around this place. Folks look forward to her visits."

I looked at the slave woman, who now stood upright. She lifted arthritic, feeble fingers and stroked the child's cheek. "I pray de Lard never allows you to see folkses in colors." Then she turned and disappeared between the cabins.

Her meaning lost on Kimie, she stood staring blankly after her.

The profoundness of the woman's words struck me. Something told me Kimie would grow to be a woman of remarkable quality and that life held a divine purpose for her.

CHAPTER
Fifteen

OVER THE NEXT WEEK, I JOINED KIMIE ON HER DAILY trips to the quarters. Though the people greeted her with enthusiasm, most watched me with reservations.

"Talks all fancy. Thinks she's better den us 'cause she's free," a woman said to her husband.

I attempted to brush off their whisperings and speculations the best I could, but it didn't relieve the pang that they viewed me as an outsider. Yet wasn't that what I was? Then there were others that embraced me in friendship with an eagerness to hear what it was like to be free.

On washing day, I stood in the stream with the other women washing the linens. I chatted to a woman I'd come to know as Jenny, and her friend, about my life in New York and my work in the Five Points.

Jenny scrunched up her nose at her friend. "Dat don't sound lak free to me. Why, life here is better dan starvin' to death in dat terrible place or worrying 'bout being murdered in your sleep. Least here our stomachs don't burn wid hunger. And we don't have to worry 'bout de missus or masa selling us off."

"But et ain't dat way at all plantations," her friend

Ruthy said. "Dis here place is good 'cause of de white folks dat run et. Ef dey had deir way, we'd all be free. But other plantations…" She shuddered.

"I believe there's much truth in your words. You see, in New York I'm a journalist."

"What's a j-jour-nal-ist?" asked Ruthy, bending over to soak a linen in the murky stream.

"I write stories for a newspaper. Mr. Reed, who's Miss Willow's friend and mine—"

"Friend? Nah, de way I see et, de man got a loving deep in his soul for Miss Willow. Can't help but feel sorry for him, wid Miss Willow only having eyes for dat Armstrong fellow." Jenny straightened and rubbed an ache in her lower back.

I'd been so busy my mind barely had time to dwell on Kipling, and I liked it that way. "Well, that proves how smart Mr. Reed is, doesn't it?"

"Meaning what?" Jenny's brow puckered.

"That he sees the goodness in your mistress. Mr. Reed owns a newspaper that fights for the rights of people like you and me. His work in the northern states and in the South have helped slaves throughout the country find their freedom. He has ties with great men, like Frederick Douglas and William Still. Have you heard of them?"

They nodded, their eyes bright as they devoured my words. "Miss Willow tells us all 'bout them. She say ef men lak dem stand united, slavery will come to an end," Jenny said.

"That's our belief. Men and women around the country and in Canada are giving our people a voice. All isn't lost. You keep believing in Miss Willow's teachings, and she'll guide you right."

Ruthy stood, tipped her face to the sky, and inhaled a deep breath.

"Whatcha doing, Ruthy?" Jenny frowned.

"Dreaming."

"'Bout what?"

"What et's lak to be free."

"Et scares me," Jenny said solemnly.

Ruthy dropped her head and sent a scowl her way. "Why's dat?"

"'Cause de world's a big place, I'd be guessing. And I ain't bin but three places in my life. Compared to dose places, Livingston feels lak all I can imagine free would luk lak. I can read, and I can write. I can weave de finest rugs 'round dese parts. And et's all thanks to de mistress." Jenny waded out of the river, and we followed. She dropped the linen she'd twisted until almost every last drop of moisture was out into a basket.

I dropped the shirt I'd washed into my basket with a waterlogged thud.

Ruthy bent and retrieved the shirt. "Dat shirt will take weeks to dry wid half de river still in et." Her experienced fingers wrung the shirt, sending a puddle of water scurrying over the rocks and earth to disappear into the river.

"I guess you showed me, now didn't you?" I laughed.

She grinned. "Et ain't nothin'. You keep your fingers for writing dem fine stories and nursing folkses back to health. De chores of running a home don't seem lak dey be for you. When you marry, your man's gonna have to hire one of dose free colored to keep your place cleant. Whites folkses, dey ain't as good at keeping a house lak us. Now I knowed you ain't white and all, but you kept lak dem."

"And you got de manners of a goat." Jenny frowned disapprovingly at her friend.

Ruthy's mouth unhinged and worry shone in her eyes. "Why, I don't mean no insult, Miss Ruby, I jus'…Jenny says I talk too much."

"Think nothing of it. I took no offense. I've enjoyed this time together."

Ruthy shook her head. "See, now you gotta go saying dose sort of things and…well, dere ain't nothin' fun 'bout evvyday work."

"Helpless, aren't I." I held up my hands in surrender.

We all laughed. I placed my basket on my hip while they hoisted theirs to balance on their heads. Together we climbed the bank to the work yard. Jenny broke out in song. I was unfamiliar with the song at first but soon caught on to the lyrics and chanted out the tune with the others. The voices of the other women from the river joined ours as they fell into step around me.

The power behind their belief in the lyrics they sang brought tears to my eyes. Chains could not keep them down. Masters could not break their spirit. In song, they rejoiced a day of anticipated freedom. In them, the beauty of the human spirit was alive. This beautiful race the whites called "Negro" were my people. Pride pounded in my chest, and I stomped the ground with conviction as we marched into the working yard.

CHAPTER
Fifteen

I saw Willow standing observing me from the doorway of the forge. Her eyes were hooded, as if she pondered on something troublesome. Behind her, *he* stood, peering over her shoulder. From afar the blacksmith studied me with confused interest.

My heart sped up.

Does he recognize me?

A thickness constricted my throat, and I hurried my steps across the yard. *Coward,* I screamed inside.

I'd walked by the stables a few days back and paused, my heart telling me to approach the man who stood within, but I considered Willow's words of caution. In the shadows of the stables he'd peered over the horse he was attending to, his brow furrowing when our eyes met. Fear overtook me, and I'd turned away and made haste back to the quarters.

At night when I lay alone in the cabin, listening to the owl that perched high in the oak tree, I thought of him. When I couldn't sleep, I'd walk down to the dock and sit, gazing out over the river. Closing my eyes, I'd concentrate on the lulling sound of the Ashley River flowing past. Wind chattered in the trees lining the riverbank while the melody of night creatures calmed my inner torment. The chiming of the blacksmith's hammer echoed as he worked long into the night. I wondered if it was his way of blocking out memories of his past.

One evening, on my way from the kitchen house, I'd glimpsed him coming out of the forge. Terror had thundered in my chest, and I'd hidden behind the privy. He walked past me within arm's reach, and I'd shrunk against the building, holding my breath, tears streaming down my cheeks. *Father?* my mind cried out. *Is it you?* My feet rooted to the ground and he walked on.

Willow had come out on the back gallery, and I'd spied on them. They laughed and chatted as if life had given them many of those special moments. Envy had stirred in my heart. But fear of rejection and worry that our theory about him being my father was inaccurate kept me hidden.

That night I'd cried myself to sleep.

"Here, help me wid dis." Jenny held out a sheet. I set my basket on the ground and took one end and helped her pin it on the line.

"Looks lak somepin' done gone and caught your mind," Ruthy said.

Not wanting to divulge our speculations about the blacksmith being my father, I said, "I was thinking—with Miss Willow's permission, of course—would you ladies allow me to write your stories? I'm writing a collection of stories from slaves throughout the United States."

"Ladies!" Ruthy snorted as if put out by the reference, but a pleased expression quickly crept across her face.

"What kind of stories dat be?" Jenny asked.

"I want to write about your hardships. What gives you strength to keep fighting. If you were free, what would you do with your life. Those sorts of things."

"But why?"

"Because I believe the stories of our people and the oppression and prejudice forced on them needs to be recorded. Future generations need to know the injustices imposed on us. We must never allow them to forget."

Jenny's lip trembled, and tears pooled in her eyes. "I'm sorry."

"For what?" I frowned.

"'Cause I judged you," she said. "When Miss Willow put you up in de marriage cabin, my heart hardened wid anger at you and her. I thought you were a traitor to de rest of us. Strolling de grounds wid Miss Willow in your purty clothes and talkin' all fancy lak."

"I reckon I'm guilty of dose feelings, too." Ruthy lowered her head.

"Please don't be too hard on yourselves. I can't say I wouldn't pass the same judgment if I were you."

They looked at me, their faces pleading for my understanding.

"I'm happy you gave me a chance."

"Well, you've proved yourself by helping out 'round de place. We figured you ain't too bad after all, ain't dat right, Jenny." Ruthy nudged her in the arm.

"Reckon so." She grinned.

I glanced around the grounds. "There's something about this place that gives me a feeling of kinship. Though

Livingston is a slave-driven plantation and I do understand you aren't truly free, there is a peacefulness about the place."

"Dis place kind of has a way of growing on ya," Jenny said.

"Think I'd miss de place ef I ever left," Ruthy added, placing her hands on her narrow hips.

"Well, ef we are luking to finish our tasks for de day, we best git dese linens hung."

I bent and retrieved a linen from my basket.

"Willow!" Whitney bellowed from the back gallery.

I straightened with the poorly squeezed linen in my hand as Willow exited the building and strolled toward the house. I watched her for a moment until…the afternoon air filled with the nostalgic tune. The black knight's tune. I turned my head in the direction of the sound. The blacksmith's shop and all that stretched out around me faded away…

Then an image flashed into my mind—a man with skin the same shade as mine, holding me on his lap. We were in a cabin packed with others like us. My head rested against his shoulder; I wore a stained cotton shift. My bare feet—small, young child's feet—draped over his knees. I felt safe surrounded by the tenderness of his arms.

Then from low in his throat, he sang the words:

Fly, my little angel,
spread your wings and soar.
Above the trees may you find freedom,
a slave no more.

The words became clear, and my lips moved in

memory. Then I was standing in a cotton field, and the blacksmith stood over me. He bandaged my fingers—bloodied from the cotton burrs—with strips of fabric. A bellow came from a man with a whip as he moved between rows. A loud crack ripped through the air, and the blacksmith winced under the lash. He teetered on his feet but remained upright.

"Get to work, nigger, or she'll be next."

"Yes, Masa," he said. His dark eyes captured mine. The man carried on down the rows. The blacksmith's eyes roved around, and he swiftly transferred some of his cotton into the bag strapped over my shoulders.

"No, Papa," I cried.

"Shh. De masa gonna whip you ef you don't meet your quota."

Hot tears raced over my cheeks. "But Papa—" I whispered.

"Hush now. Keep your head down and move," he said, and softly began to hum the tune.

"What is et, Miss Ruby?" Jenny gripped my arm, jerking me from the memory.

I began to shake. My legs felt as if they were going to give out, but my eyes were locked on the forge.

God help me! It was my papa. I stood frozen, the soggy linen clutched in my hands.

"Ruby." Willow stood before me now and pulled at the linen in my quivering hands.

I looked at her. "That tune…" My voice quivered.

"I know." Her eyes flickered with worry, yet her expression was determined.

"It's…the tune that's haunted me." Her face blurred as the tears came.

"Come with me." She handed the linen to Ruthy or Jenny; I wasn't sure. She took my hand and pulled me toward the forge.

No, I'm not ready. Fear rushed through me. I dug my heels into the ground to slow our advance toward all I'd ever wanted. "Where are we going?" I blabbered.

"To meet the one you've been searching for," Willow said.

I dug my heels deep into the ground, skidding to a halt, and grabbed at her arms. "I don't know. I can't do this. I need more time," I pleaded.

She lifted a hand and cupped my cheek. "Life has stolen enough time from you." Her eyes swam with tears. Conflict and sadness warred on her face.

"I can't," I said again.

"You must."

I glanced from her to the forge and back to her.

She slipped her arm around my waist and slowly led me forward.

What if he turns me away?

As we stepped into the forge, I beheld the man—the keeper of the tune.

"Jimmy," Willow whispered.

His whistling ceased as he turned to us. "Ah, Miss Willie. Somepin' I can help you wid?"

"I—I wanted you to meet Ruby. I believe…we think…" She looked at me; her fingers tightened on my waist. I felt the trembling of her body. Heard the pain in her voice as she said with unwavering assurance, "This is Mag."

He dropped the tool he held. His face drained of color.

"I thought…we suspected she was your Mag. But we are certain of this now." I heard fear in her voice.

"How?" His gaze turned from her to me.

"The tune you were whistling," I said. "I remember it. It's haunted me every day of my life. I remember Olivia's eyes. Her voice. The swamps. The dogs. The ship. All of it." I took a deep breath and looked into his eyes. "…and *you.*"

"Miss Willie, I asked…I tole you…" He turned and leaned his hands on the workbench. "It ain't possible. My gal is daid, gone, I tell ya." Tears labored in his voice and his shoulders sloped forward. His eyes closed and silent tears etched his cheeks.

I swallowed down the badgering in my brain telling me to run. To leave before he rejected me—I couldn't bear it.

Willow gave me a gentle nudge.

My feet crept forward despite the protesting inside me. I cast a glance over my shoulder at her. She gave me an encouraging nod.

I stood beside him, unsure what I should do or say. His body trembled, and I lifted a hand and touched his shoulder. He stiffened. And I flinched.

But something pressed me forward.

"Papa…"

He straightened, his face never lifting.

The need to touch him to make sure he wasn't a dream pulled me closer, and I raised a hand to stroke his cheek. A gasp came from him.

"Is et you…" Tears poured from him.

"I am Mag."

In the silence that fell between us, I heard the rustling of Willow's skirt as she turned and walked out without another word.

His jaw locked and his expression hardened. "Turn."

"What?" I gawked in confusion.

"Ef you're my gal, you'll have de mark."

"What mark?" I turned as instructed.

His fingers pulled back the edge of my head rag, and he bent my left ear forward. A sob escaped him. "Sweet Jesus…you've found mussy on Ol' Jimmy."

I turned back to him. "Is it there?"

He nodded, his body trembling. "Y-you're Magnolia."

Magnolia.

"And you be my gal."

He gathered me into his arms, and the familiarity of his scent came rushing back to me. Horses, smoke, and leather provided a haven of safety, and I melted into my papa's arms.

CHAPTER
Sixteen

I LEFT THE FORGE THAT DAY CHANGED. FOR YEARS I'D thought if only I'd borne the brand of a master, I'd have a connection to my past. Little did I know that an anchor-shaped mark behind my left ear would be the proof my birth father would need that I was his daughter.

After I'd left the forge, I'd gone to the main house requesting to speak to Willow, but her handmaiden had said she'd gone to her chambers with a headache. All the next day I'd not seen her around the grounds. When I saw Mr. Hendricks saddling his horse, I'd approached him and inquired about Willow's well-being. He'd informed me she was doing better. Yet she never made her rounds that day either.

The next evening—my papa didn't stay at the forge after his daily tasks were done—a rap sounded on the cabin door.

I took one last look in the mirror, thankful for the head rag that concealed my hair. My eyes were alive with excitement. Turning away, I ran my hands over the bodice of my yellow dress and adjusted the plates laid out on the table before going to the door.

The door squeaked in protest as I opened it. At the

sight of my papa's retreating back, my breath caught.

He swung back at the sound, his eyes wide. "I thought maybe you changed your mind." He wiped his palms on his trousers and inched forward.

"I've been looking forward to this all day. Please come in." I stepped back and opened the door wide.

His boots scuffed the ground as he moved forward, his eyes shifting about as if he was reconsidering.

Nerves twisted my stomach. I'd spent the afternoon in the kitchen house with Henrietta, preparing the meal spread out on the table.

Papa stepped into the cabin.

"Take a seat wherever you like," I said, and closed the door.

He stood, unmoving. "Luks lak you been working hard."

"Yes, Henrietta was most kind and helped me prepare this meal. I'm not the best cook, and my mother is far worse—a horrible teacher, in fact."

"Can't git much better dan Miss Rita's cooking."

"So I hear."

He looked sideways at me. "You happy in New York?"

"Yes; I have a wonderful life, fulfilling in many ways."

"No husband?"

"Sit, and I'll tell you anything you want to know." I placed a hand on his back, and he stiffened. He moved to the table and pulled out a chair and sat down. I sat beside him.

"Can I give you some?" I reached for his bowl, and he nodded. I ladled two spoons of fish stew into the bowl and handed it to him before serving myself.

He eyed me as he lifted his spoon and took a bite. I'd learned in our brief interactions since our reunion that he was a man of few words. Human touch made him nervous, and he felt at ease among the horses.

"I do not have a husband. But it's something I want very much, along with children."

"Ain't no man dat's caught your heart?"

"There is, but it's something that can't be." I stared into my bowl, allowing my thoughts to drift to Kipling. With most of his time being spent at his family's plantation, I missed him.

He sat silently, waiting for me to go on.

"There has been one man for a time, but we can never be together."

He waited.

"You see...he loves another. And he is white, and I'm...well, me. I suppose his kindness and his unprejudiced views of people and his fairness made me fall for him. I refuse to spend my life pining after him. I've resigned myself to forget the matter, if that is at all possible," I said solemnly.

"De man you speak of is Miss Willie's friend, Mr. Reed, ain't it?"

"Yes, but how did you know?"

"You said you work wid him at de newspaper place. You made de journey here wid him. And I seed de way he luks at Miss Willie. De boy loves de gal."

"But he can never have her...nor I him."

"Life ain't easy. Et holds lots of hurts, but et ain't

meant to be lived alone.

"After your mother died and de masa sold you, I stopped living. Thought I'd curl up and die. When I was sold to de plantation in Georgia, I tried to do away wid myself a few times, but de Lard wouldn't let me go. De masa got tired of et and thought he'd best be gittin' some coin from me 'fore he had no investment at all.

"Masa tied me to a rope behind his horse and was taking me to be sold when a lone rider rode up on de most beautiful horse I'd ever laid eyes on. Masa stopped to talk to him. De man pulled his horse up beside me, held out his riding crop, and lifted my chin to luk at him. Dere was somepin' in his eyes...a pain I recognized. An ache for somepin' lost to him.

"He offered my masa a price twice my worth. But Masa refused. A deep rumble came from deep in de rider's throat, and his jaw locked real hard lak. Den he offered double dat amount. From de corner of my eye, I seed de masa light up lak he'd stuck a vein of gold."

"What happened?"

"Course he took de monies and released me into de man's possession."

"Who was this new master?"

His eyes softened with reverence. "Mr. Charles Hendricks." He folded his hands on the table. "De day I came to Livingston, Miss Willie was but a small child. She ran out to greet her pa and den she luked up at me wid big innocent eyes and said, to her pa, 'Why does he luk so sad?' I don't recall what Masa Hendricks said. But Miss Willie, she got dis luk in her eyes—de one she gits when she ain't gonna listen no matter what ya say—and she slipped her li'l hand in mine and says, 'Don't you worry, Mister, you'll lak dis place, and I'll come to visit you evvy day.' And jus' lak dat, Miss Willie's bin pesterin' me ever since." His chuckle was loud and infectious and drowned out the emptiness I felt over the fatherly affection he held for Willow. Immersed in the heartiness of his laugh—one like no other—I smiled.

"You love her, don't you?"

"After Masa Hendricks brought me here, I learnt to live again. At fust, I was put in de fields, but den Miss Willie convinced her pa dat I needed to be wid the horses, lak she knowed dose critters is where I'm meant to be. And true to her word, each day, Miss Willie came to seek me out at de stables or forge and followed me around. Her chatter and company soothed de pain." Tears welled in his eyes. "She was my fair-skinned Magnolia."

I slipped my hand across the table to cover his, and my tears came freely. "I believed I'd been granted my one miracle in life. One is blessed to receive one, but two…" I swept my fingers across my cheek to brush away my tears. "Each day I will thank God for the day Mr. Hendricks found you. And I thank Him for giving you Willow to mend the emptiness in your heart. Without the Hendrickses, we'd never be sitting here now. I'll always remember what they've done for us. God has not forsaken us."

His face fell, and his shoulders curled forward.

"Papa?"

"I was right awful to de gal. She came to me in de middle of de night wid de notion she may have found you.

I know I hurt her. I was angry and scared to stir around in de past. I'd done de best I could to forgit. To hear your name or to think on your ma, et...et grieved me so. I didn't want to forgit you, but I had to. Ef I was gonna live, I had to block you out. Den Miss Willie wiggled et out of me one day, 'bout you and Nellie. I didn't want to forgit, you understand. Right?" His pained eyes searched mine.

"Yes, Papa. One must do what is required to survive. If life has taught me one thing, it is that we are fighters, and we will prevail."

"Dat what Miss Willie keep saying."

"Beautiful and wise. Maybe that is why she has secured the hearts of great men." I laughed.

"'Bout de heart...et be best to let dose feelin's for Mr. Reed go to de wayside. Find yourself a man dat can give you all his heart."

"A sprinkling of wisdom you and my parents share in common," I said, my thoughts running to Saul's proposal. "There is another man..."

"Well, I'll be, gal." He shook his head with a grin.

My cheeks heated. "H-his name's Saul, and he's the chief editor at the *Manhattan Observer* where I work. He declared his love for me before I left New York." Avoiding his gaze, I picked at the crumbs wedged between the planks of the table. "He's a good man and would make a worthy husband."

"But you don't love him," he said.

"In time...I believe I could learn to."

"I didn't love your ma at first."

"No?" I lifted my head to look at him.

He shook his head. "Bin shy since I was a youngster. Never much cared to have a wife. Learnt from watching others dat ef a masa ain't got nothin' to hold over you, dey can't hurt you. I did my work as I was tole and kept to myself. When de masa put Nellie and me together for breeding, I hid from her. But not for long—your ma, she sought me out and tole me I warn't her fust man, and she'd teach me all dat went on between a man and a woman. I was scared—oh my, was I scared." He laughed at the memory. "But she won my trust, and made me a man." His cheeks flushed. "I learnt to love dat woman wid evvy bit of me.

"Den came de day we found out she was wid child, and a fear lak we'd never felt 'fore grew in us. By our bed at night, we prayed to *her* Gawd dat you'd be born a boy. He didn't answer dat pray, and I was angry wid Him. Den when I lost my Nellie after de masa whipped her so badly she never recovered, de anger festered in me. When he took de rest dere was to me by selling you, I cursed Gawd dat day for forsaking me. After dat, I became daid inside.

"You see, Mag, it ain't right, what I said to de Lard, and dat's somepin' I aim to make right—ef he'll hear me. Dose days wid your ma and you were 'bout as happy a life a slave can have. A family's what makes life worth livin'."

Together in that marriage cabin, we chatted long into the night about my life in New York and the decision that lay ahead of me. I heeded his words. After all, what was life if you didn't have someone to share it with?

Epilogue

New York

O N A SATURDAY MORNING THAT SPRING, THE CARRIAGE stopped in front of a brick two-storey home in the black village in uptown Manhattan. The congestion and noise of the city had faded away into the serenity of farmland. I glanced with pride around the small village, first established in 1825, two years before the enslaved people of New York were emancipated. I'd gone to church and was enrolled in school in the community. Black people with financial means could purchase land here, and some landowners even earned the right to vote.

The driver opened the carriage door and lowered the step. For a moment I sat still to quell the nerves roiling my stomach, inhaling the fresh air not befouled with factory smoke.

"Miss," the driver said, holding out a hand to assist me. I laid my gloved hand in his and disembarked.

Gripping the sides of my gown, I ascended the steps to the front door. I didn't knock. Instead I paced the landing, hands clasped together to stop the trembling.

You need to do this before you lose your nerve.

I lifted the bronze knocker and rapped three times, then stepped back. Sweat dampened the inside of my gloves, and I glanced back at the carriage.

The instinct to flee rose, and I turned. *What am I doing? I can't—*

The door opened, and I froze.

"Miss Stewart? What a surprise," his rich voice said. I spun on my heel to find Saul in the doorway. His dark flesh glistened against his crisp white shirt. My stomach fluttered.

"I-I'm...are your parents home?" I finally blurted.

"Mother is. Have you come to see her?" Puzzlement shone in his eyes.

"Well...no. I wanted to make sure someone was."

His brow furrowed.

"You see," I rushed on, "I've come to see you. But seeing as I'm showing up uninvited, I wanted my visit to be proper because I wouldn't want anyone thinking—"

"Ruby." He used my name for the first time in all the years I'd known him.

I stopped, my eyes resting on his lips. Goose pimples blossomed over my flesh. The way he said my name revealed a yearning that came from deep within the giant man. "Yes," I whispered.

"Did you travel all the way out here to blabber on my front step?"

"No...However, I do wish to speak to you, but somewhere more private."

"Come, we will go to the garden." He took my hand in his and led me down the corridor to a set of garden doors that opened onto a lush garden.

My heart hammered and fear surged through me. What would he think of me coming out here? What would he think of what I had to say?

The heels of my shoes clicked over the stone pathway as he led me through a wooden archway entangled with green vines to a seating area. "Please, take a seat." He gestured to the wrought iron bench nestled in a forest of blossoming cherry trees. He took a seat beside me and turned to face me, his long legs touching my knees.

I laughed nervously at the image. Resting my hands in my lap, I released a calming breath and pushed on with what had brought me here. "While I was away I had a lot of time to think. I've considered your proposal for courtship, and I've come to a conclusion," I said. Looking into his eyes, I found the reassurance to go on. "I would be delighted to accept your proposal."

His breath caught. Then a smile touched his eyes. He lifted a hand and his palm cupped my cheek. "The finest among woman you are, Ruby Stewart."

I leaned into the warmth of his palm. The gentleness of his touch and the love in his eyes filled me with certainty. *Yes, I will come to love this man.* I'd devote my life to being a good wife.

His head lowered and I arched my neck to receive the earnestness of his kiss. And found a wholeness I'd searched for all my life.

COMING SOON:

THE MASTER OF SHIPS

NOVELLA TWO

Pre-order Available

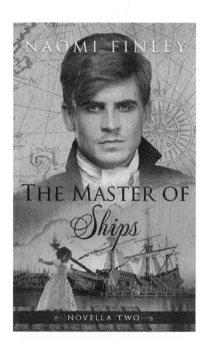

ABOUT
the Author

Naomi is a bestselling and award-winning author living in Northern Alberta. She loves to travel and her suitcase is always on standby awaiting her next adventure. Naomi's affinity for the Deep South and its history was cultivated during her childhood living in a Tennessee plantation house with six sisters. Her fascination with history and the resiliency of the human spirit to overcome obstacles are major inspirations for her writing and she is passionately devoted to creativity. In addition to writing fiction, her interests include interior design, cooking new recipes, and hosting dinner parties. Naomi is married to her high school sweetheart and she has two teenage children and two dogs named Ginger and Snaps.

Sign up for my newsletter: authornaomifinley.com/contact

Made in the USA
San Bernardino, CA
11 June 2019